I'M SO OCD

I'M SO OCD

I'M SO OCD

Asher Feltman

Cherish
EDITIONS

First published in Great Britain 2023 by Cherish Editions
Cherish Editions is a trading style of Shaw Callaghan Ltd & Shaw Callaghan 23
USA, INC.
The Foundation Centre
Navigation House, 48 Millgate, Newark
Nottinghamshire NG24 4TS UK
www.triggerhub.org
Text Copyright © 2023 Asher Feltman

British Library Cataloguing in Publication Data
A CIP catalogue record for this book is available upon request
from the British Library
ISBN: 978-1-913615-96-3
This book is also available in the following eBook formats:
ePUB: 978-1-913615-97-0

Cover design by More Visual
Typeset by Lapiz Digital Services

CONTENTS

INTRODUCTION

It is my privilege to work with individuals who are burdened with mental illness. The medical field's knowledge of the brain and its myriad functions and dysfunctions continues to evolve. With more knowledge and experience in hand, better interventions emerge. Despite this progress, mental illness continues to afflict individuals, and the treatments are not necessarily curative, pleasant or even helpful for some. Treatments well studied and established are frequently unavailable as a result of inaccessibility, financial costs and/or the dizzying maze of hoops and authorizations required. Some who have access are not able to engage. And of those who do access and engage, many must often still struggle through a foreign and harrowing treatment process to realize improvements.

Just because you have a mental illness, such as obsessive compulsive disorder, does not mean you are void of feelings, memories, ambition and desires. The presence of a mental illness does not negate that an individual is a person, a human being, with all the parts and pieces that make them who they are.

It is my privilege to know Ash and participate in his life experience. Ash is an individual with a ragingly severe mental illness who, despite staggeringly atypical neurological function, persevered. He rode the tsunami, the ups and downs, the ins and outs. Whether he had additional visits with the doctor, extra therapy sessions, more inpatient or day treatment, medication added to his pharmacopeia, or just another hour, day, week or month of torture inside the illness, Ash maintained. When the practitioner or system failed, ignored or dismissed him, he did not jump ship or bail. Ash utilized his internal and external resources and emerged "through the eye of a needle."

His story is beautiful, inspirational, educational and hopeful.

Roger Robinson, M.D.

FOREWORD

You are about to read a story about one young man's journey
through the labyrinth of obsessive compulsive disorder (OCD).
While not a professional in the field, Asher Feltman, at 29 years old,
has had a virtual lifetime of personal experience in the treatment
and management of OCD. His story, written with painful honesty,
humor and poignancy, represents a roadmap of the challenges and
struggles those with this disorder face every day.

This book should be read by anybody who has experienced the
challenges of dealing with OCD or has a loved one coping with the
disorder. Though not a treatment manual, Asher presents a wealth of
information regarding the variety of therapeutic resources available
in prose that is highly readable and understandable.

OCD is defined by the presence of obsessions and/or compulsions.
Obsessions are persistent and unwanted thoughts, images or urges.
Compulsions are repetitive behaviors that one feels driven to perform,
often in response to an obsession. Almost everyone has experienced
mild OCD behavior. Checking repeatedly that you've locked the door
or turned off the oven are examples. Common superstitions, such as
crossing one's fingers or not stepping on cracks, can be considered
OCD-like. However, these behaviors rise to the level of a disorder
only when they severely impact the social, emotional or occupational
functioning of the individual.

In his story, Asher details the struggles and efforts he underwent to
deal with the scope and severity of his OCD symptoms. Asher's story
will continue as he pursues his personal and professional goals and
utilizes the strategies that allow him to manage his OCD throughout

his life. His book ends not only with a description of these coping strategies, but with the belief that hope plays an essential role in handling adversity in coping with mental illness or any life challenge.

Bruce J. Abel, Ph.D.

CHAPTER 0: I'M SO OCD

"I'm so OCD."

You've heard somebody say these words before. Maybe you've said them. Let's call it probable. It's okay. I'm not mad. But what I am, really, is OCD.

Like, *actually* OCD. I have obsessive compulsive disorder.

This doesn't mean that my room has to be clean, or that I feel a project isn't complete until it's perfect – much to the annoyance of my co-workers. I don't sit and rearrange items on my desk until they're in just the right spot. I don't get frustrated and thoughtlessly utter, "I'm so OCD," when I wash my hands.

There's obviously nothing wrong with having a tidy home. Or striving for "perfection," whatever that may mean to you. Having an organized workspace is definitely a point of pride. And hygiene is obviously important. But complaining about any of these things, and having those three words – "I'm so OCD" – accompany these human behaviors? It just isn't OCD.

The thing about OCD is we've all got a little bit of it in us. OCD's partner in crime, anxiety, is there too. Nobody likes to feel anxious, but we all feel it. While the human psyche does all it can not to acknowledge negative thoughts, feelings and emotions, anxiety is inevitable and inescapable.

At its core, obsessive compulsive disorder *is* anxiety. It's that scary emotion, that weightless feeling right in your chest that everyone has felt. But when you have OCD – actual OCD – this anxiety isn't something that causes you to feel "down" at its weakest, or perhaps to have a "bad day" at its worst. OCD anxiety is defined as anxiety that affects your quality of life.

At least that's how I see it. Because, even in the medical golden age we live in, there are things in the world of health that we still have no idea how to comprehend.

Everyone currently out from under their rocks knows all about the evil that is cancer. Cancer is horrible. But you *see* cancer. It has tangible, visible results. Diabetes does, too. I know that very well. My older brother deteriorated to skeletal form in the fifth grade before receiving his Type 1 diabetes diagnosis. It was plain to see something was wrong with a previously healthy, active young boy.

Mental illness does not have visible results. There is no physical manifestation. You don't see people think, after all. As human beings, we need to see something to believe it. And if we don't see it, we have trouble believing. The proof is in the pudding, as nobody ever really says.

This is why people like me, who suffer from a mental illness, usually keep it bottled up. Nobody really understands. Even family. And if you try to explain yourself, you might as well try and explain what Disney's plans were for *Star Wars* Episodes 7, 8 and 9.

Credible or not, cries for help tend to sound like a convenient excuse to "get out" of things, or shirk responsibilities, or avoid working hard, or… the list goes on and on.

You just can't *see* a mental illness. Even after my diagnosis in 2007, which came a year after staying at a hospital wing that treated youth eating disorder patients because my parents and a carousel of doctors had no idea what was wrong with me, it was so hard to ask for help. Even for my mom and dad, it was hard to ask.

To this day, I will disguise my worries and hide things from those closest to me. Do they want to help? Of course. But again, you explain how Disney's ace in the hole was Palpatine's resurrection.

Obsessive compulsive disorder is not a uniform disease. It reveals itself in many forms. The most common are the ones that draw the "I'm so OCD" exclamations I hear oh so often: organization, perfectionism, or something along the lines of needing things in an exact spot or a task done a certain way.

The other well-known version revolves around cleanliness: excessive hand-washing or showering, or anything to keep clean.

There are so many versions of this cruel disease, but mine has everything to do with thinking. I have what are called intrusive thoughts. If I think about something that I don't like, not only does it cause me distress, anxiety, worries, etc., but I will go to great lengths to rid myself of both the thought and the accompanying bad feelings.

It sounds innocent enough, but while the intrusive thoughts are the "obsession," or the "O" in OCD, those specific lengths I go to are the "compulsions," also called rituals, and they are the "C" in OCD. They can last seconds, but they can also last hours. Or even an entire day. Or more.

I remember days when I would wake up to an unpleasant thought, not knowing how to handle it, and then give up and decide that the entire day was lost to my anxiety. Not until I slept again could I "reset" the cycle.

The thing about thinking is we are *always* doing it. And it's hard to *not* think, especially about things we don't want to think about. Take the pink elephant example.

Ready? Okay. Don't think about a pink elephant.

If you aren't visualizing the color pink, an elephant, or the whole pink elephant, I'm quite impressed.

For me, my obsessions were all about people. Out of respect for those who unknowingly and unwittingly caused me so much suffering over the years, they will never be named in this book. Never. I'm going to avoid specifics like I currently avoid rituals.

I wish I could truly tell all, but the reality is that I have been caused terrible distress by ordinary people. Something about the way they looked, acted or perhaps treated me, made them a target for my anxiety. Many who caused me pain never even spoke a word to me. But they don't know that.

If you feel at all like I'm omitting key elements of the story, please don't. My parents don't even know everything. Some of it is so ridiculous that it would only serve to humiliate me and others for no good reason.

What would happen to me, over and over, day after day – really, moment by moment – is my rituals would become so long that I would get what my dad eventually called "stuck."

I was basically frozen. Paralyzed. And it happened when I had to do straightforward tasks like getting out of bed, getting in the shower or exiting the car before school – heck, if we even got that far in high school, it was a good morning. Every single thing I did was at the mercy of my thoughts. And they never stopped.

Unfortunately for me, but worse for my dad who was in charge of getting me from bed to school each morning, this process was laborious and exhausting, and, worst of all, it destroyed my relationship with him.

I'm happy to report it has since been more than repaired. As have I.

But back then, I would get stuck at every task. When – or often if – I got to school, I was reliant on the special education program to simply get through the day. I wanted so badly to be in class, to have some sense of normalcy, but I would get stuck so often that my entire time in a classroom was spent ritualizing. And being around people only made it worse. The controlled special ed environment at least got me through some days.

The hardest part of all of this, and the hardest thing for me to grasp as a tormented kid, is the realization that diseases like OCD, or cancer, or diabetes, have no cure. Treatment? Sure. We do our best. But there is no cure. It's a part of you forever.

Thankfully, this story has a happy ending. Or as I've come to see it, a happy beginning.

So, let's put on some 90s music – I'll go ahead and pick *NSYNC – turn back the clock and tell this thing from the start.

For Mom and Dad, in no particular order

CHAPTER 1

1993 – BIRTH

Asher Grant Feltman was born on May 29, 1993.

CHAPTER 2

1994–2000 – CHILDHOOD

I have to admit that having a mental illness makes for quite a story, hence me writing this book. Before I got sick, there was nothing too remarkable about my childhood. Was I an awesome kid? Sure. Did I have a good home? Absolutely. Was I cute as Jonathan Lipnicki in *Jerry Maguire*? You know it. (Am I as jacked as he is now? Unfortunately not.)

By all accounts, I had a normal childhood. This isn't really the interesting part of my story. But hey, it's my book. I might not get another shot at this.

As a kid, my world pretty much revolved around sports. My lifestyle was built around my love of the game, those games being baseball and basketball. Baseball was and still is my favorite sport, but as far as rooting interests, my every moment depended on whether the Dallas Mavericks were playing well.

I caution against any form of idolization, but kids need to have heroes. And mine was Dirk Nowitzki.

There were others. I took a liking to Texas Rangers utilityman Frank Catalanotto. As a player, he was everything I wanted to be. A good teammate, coachable, could play any position on the diamond, and his unique left-handed swing inspired me to learn how to switch-hit and then primarily become a lefty hitter. (Not a lot of kids throw left-handed, so youth switch-hitters don't hit righty much.)

As a kid, I would dress in a full baseball uniform when I went to Rangers games. Every morning, I cut the previous day's box scores

out of the newspaper and taped them to my bedroom walls, the inside
of drawers, and put leftovers in a binder for safekeeping.

I had jerseys of players from all over the MLB and the NBA. I
loved my hometown teams, but I was really just a fan of the game.
I collected memorabilia, was first in line for autographs, and came
home from baseball games with a backpack full of foul balls and
basketball games with somebody's sweaty headband.

My dad took me to Rangers games right as the gates opened so I
could chase players around in batting practice. We would go to Mavs
games just as early, after our signature trip to Sal's Pizza on Wycliff
Avenue, so I could get autographs and see these larger-than-life
athletes up close.

During our spring break trips to Arizona, my dad and brother
would spend the day golfing. But before they hit the course, they
would drop me off at the ballpark and let me loose. Until proven
otherwise, I maintain that heaven is spring training baseball in
Arizona.

We took family trips every summer to different ballparks around
the country. With friends of my brothers and their fathers and sons, I
got to see Fenway Park in Boston, Coors Field in Colorado, Olympic
Stadium in Montreal, Petco Park in San Diego, Camden Yards in
Baltimore, and my favorite of all, Pac Bell Park in San Francisco.

You could say, with a pinch of irony, that I was obsessed.

And obsessed I was, perhaps to a fault. I had little interest in
anything else. But if something was in second place, it was comic
books. I loved to read, but in another ironic twist, a short attention
span made it hard to digest novels. Plus, my parents had no interest in
film or fiction, so there wasn't a lot of exposure to such things.

Once I did discover comic books, my interest in superheroes
started to grow. Not to the point it is today – where superheroes
have replaced sports as my, well, obsession – but the seeds were
nevertheless planted at a pretty young age.

It was a childhood without many problems. I had friends over all
the time, and we played wiffle ball, turning my backyard into Fenway
Park with the way my house protruded outward toward the back. We

even played baseball *in the house*, scuffing up the walls and frustrating my parents and siblings.

We played basketball in the driveway all night. My dad put an extra light out there and even painted a half-court on the concrete. (He probably got tired of us using chalk.)

We had *Madden*, *NBA Live* and *MVP Baseball* video game tournaments. We watched movies in our sleeping bags until we finally went to sleep. It was all a "normal" childhood.

There were some things that weren't perfect. I didn't really understand my brother's diabetes, but I recall how much it impacted our family. At the hospital my brother was in, I remember playing inside a giant Dallas Cowboys helmet with my cousin Harris. I remember my brother keeping a food journal and my parents checking off everything he ate and drank. I remember his low blood sugar episodes more than anything. But I didn't feel the impact of *his* disease on my life.

My sister? We joke that she's the "normal" one. As long as her *Gilmore Girls* episodes went uninterrupted, she was harmless. But try to turn a game on before Rory's episodic arc reached its conclusion and there'd be hell to pay. As confrontational as sharing the TV could be, and as foreign as that seems now in a world of streaming devices, my sister and I made up for any bad blood by bonding over *That '70s Show*.

While my childhood was pretty conventional, there were signs of my future if you looked for them. I was extremely meticulous, even as a kid. Though my obsessions were innocent – sports, Spider-Man, *Star Wars* – they were nonetheless obsessive. Even for fun hobbies and life's enjoyment, I devoted a lot of time and energy to anything I did.

Fortunately, those things were all pretty great.

CHAPTER 3
2000–2005 – ADOLESCENCE

Because of my midyear May birthday, I was held back in kindergarten. It was either that or I couldn't stop wetting my pants. The second one is funnier.

I went to a private Jewish school for my dual kindergarten terms, then followed my brother and sister to public school. Judaism has always been important in my family, but the Feltmans identify as Reform Jews, and going to a Jewish school wasn't as important as being exposed to the diversity of public school.

I kept going to Hebrew school on Wednesdays to prepare for my Bar Mitzvah at age 13, but I'm grateful for the opportunity to have gone to public school while also maintaining my religion.

In 2004, *Spider-Man 2* came out. My good friend Pierce and I saw it in theaters on opening day. Then we went again that same day. And again the next day. And again. I fondly remember seven trips in the first week.

When we weren't at the theater, we were playing one-on-one basketball in my backyard to 100 – yes, we really did this and kept score by hand – or using the cul-de-sac in front of his house to play wiffle ball with our friends.

Life was good. It was easy. I never worried about needing food, shelter, love from my family or companionship from friends, and at this point, I was even getting the girls! It was like a professional athlete winning Rookie of the Year, and then falling into obscurity.

Of the many memories I made with friends, Pierce once again comes to mind. During the long, hot days of summer, we started to pursue our musical talents while we hung out by the pool. He and I came up with two songs: "Chlorine" and "Poo Water."

The writing process was short and sweet. Each song literally has one line.

"Chlorine" by Pierce Ryan and Asher Feltman
I like the smell of chlorine… Oh yeah, oh baby.

"Poo Water" by Pierce Ryan and Asher Feltman
Girl, [pause] *you smell,* [pause] *like poo water.*

(There's an extra emphasis on the "o's" in poo or it doesn't work.)

Even typing this now is a little embarrassing, but I can't lie, we were (and at least one of us still is) very proud of these two hits.

The point here, at the risk of not having one and completely wasting your time, is that I had a fun childhood.

I loved to be with others, but I've cherished my alone time since I was young. Just me and my PlayStation was enough. I still love being home. I'm a notorious stress machine on family trips, even on the most relaxing of vacations.

When I was 12, I wrote a letter from summer camp begging for my parents to let me come home early. It's not that I wasn't having fun at camp, I just wanted to be home. It's one of my dad's favorite stories to tell, how I desperately bribed my parents to come pick me up and that I even offered to pay them to come get me early.

My love of movies, science fiction and also comic books really took off on May 19, 2005. On this day in history, *Star Wars: Episode III – Revenge of the Sith* was released.

My good friend Jake, who I still talk to today and literally texted a few minutes ago, held his 12th birthday party on our last day of 5th grade. There were a few firsts for yours truly that day. Jake's mom bought me my first Starbucks Frappuccino, which I blissfully thought was calorie-free like coffee for several years.

More importantly, his birthday party was an opening day showing of *Star Wars*. Oh man, my world exploded that day. I had always had an interest in superheroes and sci-fi, especially with the *Spider-Man* films that had recently come out, but I was uncultured when it came to all things *Star Wars*.

Thankfully, Jake and his family weren't. And thankfully, no longer was I.

There are moments in every human being's life that they remember forever. They define them. They shape who they are. They are the fiber of their being. This day in 2005, seeing *Revenge of the Sith*, which remains my number one movie of all time, was one of those moments.

(Before moving on, when I say a movie is my favorite of all time, it is not said carelessly. I keep a mega-list of my favorite movies ever, which has really grown in recent years as I started to drift from sports to movies as my primary source of passion, and it's just passed 700 films. There are possessions in every human's life that they hold close. They define them. They shape who they are. They are the fiber of their being. My "Infinity" list of movies is one of these things.)

Finally, at the end of 2005, I had the extreme privilege to go to Israel with my family. I returned 13 years later on a Birthright trip, and while I remember more from that trip, it has to be mentioned that I went to frickin' Israel in fifth grade. I mean, how lucky was I?

CHAPTER 4

2006, PART 1 – UH OH

It's hard to find the moment in time when I first realized something was wrong with me. It's hard for a 12-year-old to recognize something is wrong at all. At the least, I knew something was *different*.

Sometime in early 2006, I was playing *NBA Live* on my PlayStation 2, waiting for my dad to call for dinner. A normal night. When he did call, I put the game on the save screen and clicked the appropriate buttons to save my progress before I went downstairs. The problem was, when I saved my game, something didn't feel right.

If that seems rather vague, that's because it is. "Something" didn't feel "right." To this day, I couldn't tell you what it is. The best I can do is call it anxiety. A pit in my chest, a sinking feeling in my stomach that means nothing but discomfort and paralyzes you for a moment in time.

The problem was this moment became minutes. Not just that, I was saving my game over and over… and over and over… until that feeling went away. My dad called for dinner again, then my siblings took annoyed turns trying to summon me. To them, it was me being difficult, ignoring the familial call for dinner like kids have been doing for as long as there have been kids.

It was especially hard to cope with making my brother and sister angry. They were just kids, too, and my behavior on the surface came off as the third-born doing third-born things. For them, I was being a spoiled little brat and making life more difficult for them because that was my job as the youngest of three. But that wasn't the case.

For the first time, I had become "stuck," a word that would become a fixture in my life going forward. I could not move from my spot on the couch, and eventually the only way I could get up was to compensate for my anxiety with what doctors call a "tic."

The best way I can describe my first tic is that sort of gurgling sound you make to massage your throat when it's itchy. I did this to supplant the anxiety – whatever sense in the world that makes. But what we all learn about OCD eventually is that *none of it makes sense*.

I started avoiding being stuck by making this noise, but the obvious problem there is that *I was making this noise*! It was loud, awkward and disruptive, and it started to physically hurt my throat.

One of my dad's greatest hand-me-downs are his allergies. I've been on loads of allergy medicine since I was a young kid. I took allergy shots weekly for about a year to help offset the aggravation from grass, trees and pollen. You can see how that would be problematic.

I bring this up not to enlighten you on the wonders of Benadryl, but because my allergies and asthma were so bad that it made sense for my family to assume the throat-clearing was simply a side effect of allergies.

Nobody in their right mind makes the jump from throat tic to mental illness, or even anxiety. Mental illness awareness has come a long way – with still a long way to go – but in 2006, nobody knew much about OCD. And a family already dealing with a teenage diabetic had enough on their plate.

We soon realized this was more than allergies, though. Especially when my school performance cratered, my home life became joyless and unproductive, I didn't see my friends, I lost interest in my recreational sports teams, and it was a chore to move me from place to place.

Not only did the throat tic worsen, but I also started developing new habits. Just like I kept saving my game over and over, I started repeating ordinary tasks throughout the day. Opening and shutting doors became opening and shutting doors three to four times. Saying "thank you" at the dinner table became "thank you, thank you, thank you, thank you," until I got it just "right."

If I touched a doorknob, I would touch it over and over. If I turned off a water faucet, I would do it half a dozen times. Getting into bed at night was the worst. Between all the repetition, going to the bathroom, brushing my teeth and then finally climbing into bed, the process could take an hour or more.

Not to mention getting up in the morning, which was just as bad and caused many delays in the Feltman household.

When I walked, navigating the cracks in the sidewalk was no longer a fun game that many kids play. If I stepped on one, it meant stopping, going backward, retracing my steps and starting again. These things became very common, very time consuming, and very exhausting. By the end of the day, I was completely worn out. But my bedtime routine still took its usual time, and when my head finally hit the pillow, I was almost home free.

Finally shutting down and actually going to sleep was the last step. However – and I've always found this as fascinating as it is frustrating – my thoughts actually followed me into my sleep.

I had few dreams and many nightmares, often involving violent acts happening to myself or my family. It was distressing, but even worse, I had the same rituals, tics and OCD habits in my dreams that plagued me when I was awake. There was no rest. This was a 24/7 burden.

Unbeknownst to my parents, and even myself, these tics were all an effort to alleviate my worsening anxiety. My future self would learn that tics are the compulsion in OCD behavior. The problem was, I had yet to develop any debilitating obsessions. Once those started, the compulsions got to levels that I had no chance to control.

My school attendance started to become a problem. Previously, I loved going to school to see my friends. I was popular in sixth grade, I had a lot of friends, I was very social, I played sports every day after school, and I maintained a little better than B average.

Almost overnight, all that came to a screeching halt.

When my parents could actually *get me to school*, my participation was non-existent. It became clear that something bigger was happening here, and my parents started to seek medical help.

Finding a doctor for anxiety, or anything related to mental illness, is extremely difficult. It's hard to quantify what you're going through when it's all in your head, especially if you're a prepubescent teenager who doesn't share his thoughts and feelings anyway.

All of it was very overwhelming… and very expensive. That didn't register with me then, and my parents would never, ever use money as a crutch, but we saw so many doctors early on that I can barely remember their faces, although I do remember some names, for one reason or another.

One of the first doctors we saw put me on medication that saw me go from bad to worse to chaos. Medication is tricky, and there's a reason those commercials list all those side effects in one breath. My reactions to medication over the years have been inconsistent at best, volatile at worst. When he stopped answering phone calls about adjusting my meds, we moved on.

I remember Dr. Ackerman by name, only because our family knew his family. I remember Dr. Weaver because he was one of the first doctors to try and teach me to "manipulate" my thoughts, rather than control them or "get rid" of them. His idea was to give your obsessive thoughts a tangible form, like a picture. Take that picture and fold it up into pieces until it's gone. This actually started to work for me in the short term, but it was time consuming. Still… anything helped.

That May, my Bar Mitzvah was to take place. In plain terms, a Bar Mitzvah is a Jewish ceremony that celebrates a young boy becoming a man. Most people know what a Bar or Bat Mitzvah is. You've been to the parties. You've heard about the checks.

But instead of celebrating a momentous occasion in the Jewish religion, in my life and in my family's life, it was a weekend of misery. Before my Torah reading on Saturday morning, the Rabbi told the audience I was not feeling well and to excuse any clearing of the throat or noises that I made during the ceremony.

I was so embarrassed to get up on that stage. Performing is hard enough, but I felt like everyone was thinking about this mysterious noise that I was liable to make at any moment. Tics are meant to alleviate anxiety, but with the spotlight on me, I remember getting through the whole thing without one single vocal tic. I tapped all over the desk and counted every step I took, but nobody was looking for that.

That night, I spent most of my Bar Mitzvah party hiding in the back of the room. It's an odd sight to see the person a party *is for* not participating in any of the festivities. Or looking like they would rather be anywhere else. I felt the worst for my parents, who had to come up with numerous ridiculous anecdotes to try and explain my behavior.

I would escape to the bathroom whenever I could, just to be out of sight. One moment stands out in my memory above others. Everyone was having a great time, dancing and singing along with the band, except me. My friend Colby left the action to check on me in the back of the room, then took a seat on the floor next to me. My mom quickly came over and assured Colby I was alright.

"He's just resting," she probably tried to say.

Colby was and is a sharp kid. He knew something was up – my recent behavior at school and disappearance from our club basketball team was proof enough. He went back to hang out with our friends, but that moment sticks with me all these years later. I suppose Colby deserved to knock me out of our fantasy football playoffs in 2020.

After my Bar Mitzvah, my sixth-grade school year came to an unceremonious close. Looking back, it's amazing to me I didn't have to repeat any grades from sixth grade onward. For that, I credit my parents, but also so many great teachers and school administrators. They knew something was going on, and my predicament was unusual and out of place for me. They wanted me to move on through school in anticipation of this "strange thing" eventually going away.

***

I continued to see many different psychologists and take prescribed medications from my carousel of rotating psychiatrists, but nothing seemed to help. The breaking point came, of all places, at a Mavericks playoff game against the Phoenix Suns in the 2006 Western Conference Finals.

There was nothing more important to me at this time of my life than the Mavs. Them being on the brink of their first NBA Finals appearance was obviously a big deal.

All my life, going to a sports game meant staying until the bitter end. Even if the Mavericks were down 30, or if we were at a Rangers game and Chan Ho Park gave up seven runs in the first inning… we were staying. Leaving early was not an option, and I respect my dad for sticking to that over all those years of games that we absolutely should have left early.

It was either Game 4 or Game 5 of the series against the Suns, and I was really struggling. The cruelest thing about anxiety and OCD is that it attacks you when you really don't want to be bothered. And it attacks strongest when you're doing something you enjoy.

Example: If I was sitting in class and the science teacher was lecturing us on the periodic table, my mind would wander off without me caring too much. If I was at a sports game, I just wanted to watch the game, enjoy my team and be there with my dad and his friends, Kenny and Mike, but that was when the OCD would kick in.

But in this Suns series, right after sweating my way through my Bar Mitzvah, I really started to unravel. For the first time in my entire life, we left a sports game early. Not just that, we left a Western Conference Finals game early.

And we left because of me.

My dad saw how much I was struggling. Unlike my dad but *like* my mom, I wear my emotions on my sleeve. My dad is notoriously hard to read. However, on this night, when I tugged on his shoulder and said I couldn't take it anymore, I could see the pain in his eyes. As miserable and scared as I was, I can still picture the look on his face today. Seeing a similar look from Bob and Lois, Kenny's parents who were seated next to us and knew how much basketball meant to me, left a sting in my chest that I still feel right now remembering this moment.

That night, we discovered that all these doctors, all the medication, could only do so much. Shortly after, I became a patient at Children's Medical Center Dallas.

CHAPTER 5
2006, PART 2 – HOSPITALIZATION

The first thing I want to say about going to the hospital is how fortunate I am to come from a family with the means to send me to one. Medical treatment, especially for mental illnesses, is not just hard to find, but very, very expensive. Money has never been an issue for my parents when it came to getting me help. I am eternally grateful for that. On the other hand, I always think about those who suffer from mental illnesses that are becoming more common and cannot afford treatment. I really am lucky I got help. My life literally would not be mine to live if I did not get it.

After trying everything at our disposal – therapy, medicine and anything else we could think of – I was admitted to Children's Medical Center Dallas at the turn of May to June 2006. Even at a hospital designated for young people, there was no hospital wing for mental illness. At this point, we still didn't even know *what* I had.

So, I ended up in the eating disorder part of Children's, and while I don't remember a lot, I remember how eye-opening it was. I remember how strangely reassuring it was seeing other kids struggling so terribly with something. I didn't have an eating disorder, but kids are kids. We saw our struggles in each other, even if they weren't the exact same. We were all going through hell.

The primary reason for my hospitalization was to get me on stronger medicine and monitor the process. That, and to try and come up with some form of a diagnosis. Up until this point, it was just "anxiety" or "depression" or "sorry, we have no idea." Sending me to Children's was the right call, and again, I'm so thankful that it was possible for my family.

The elephant in the room when I was hospitalized was that the Mavericks had advanced to the NBA Finals. I chuckle now talking about a sports game – even if it is a championship – in the same breath as my health, but holding on to the hope and spirit the Mavs gave me was keeping me strong in a time of non-stop suffering.

I don't remember much from my time at Children's. I was on so much medication that there isn't much to remember. But certain things stick out, and over time my hospital memories have become the memories of my childhood, so I force myself to see them in a positive light.

I kept my sanity by hanging a toy hoop on my door and treating (read: bothering) everyone in the hallways with my live commentary.

"Devin Harris with the ball. He gets a screen from Dirk Nowitzki and dribbles right. He goes past Steve Nash to the basket. Shawn Marion goes for the block and Harris passes back out to Nowitzki for the open jumper. He shoots… and it's good!!!"

Picture a 13-year-old running from spot to spot in the hallway to simulate all these different players, all the while blurting out commentary as if he was the play-by-play announcer on TV. That was me. I can see how that would drive people crazy from the other side.

Another thing I'll never forget was the strict food schedule. Of course, I was surrounded by young people receiving medical care for eating disorders. This meant we ate very specific foods at certain times, and we only ate at those times. When we weren't eating, we did not discuss food.

During one of our game nights, we played the card game Apples to Apples. If you don't know, it's a word-association game played in a group. And it's pretty fun. But what I remember is the hospital staff going through all the cards before we played and removing any card that mentioned food or drink.

It's these things that stick out, but my exit from Children's was the most eventful.

The Mavericks and the Miami Heat were in the NBA Finals and the series was 3-2 Miami with Game 6 coming back to Dallas. Children's is next door to the American Airlines Center, the home of the Mavs, and I was discharged that night so I could attend the game.

It wasn't the doctor's first choice, but I put up quite the fight. My treatment was ongoing, and at that point it had been inconclusive, so my dad took me to the game. I wasn't necessarily making progress, and we were still unsure what was wrong with me.

While you could say we left prematurely, we left with a golden ticket: a new doctor.

In my final days at Children's, a parent of another patient gave us the name of a psychologist with whom they had found great success. Days later, I had an appointment with Dr. Bruce Abel, right in our hometown of Plano.

***

Of all the things to happen to me in my first year of this new life, discovering Dr. Abel had the biggest impact. It didn't feel like it at the time, and I was either belligerent or sleeping through the first several sessions, but my parents used these preliminary meetings to give him the whole story.

And for the first time, we knew exactly what ailed me: obsessive compulsive disorder.

After many months and about a dozen doctors, an official diagnosis provided my family with something, *anything*, to hold on to. It's hard to know how to fight when you don't know what you're fighting. Now, we knew what it was.

But *what was* obsessive compulsive disorder?

Dr. Abel gave us many books to read and references to utilize. My parents went to work, balancing my newfound disorder with their lives, their jobs and their two other kids, one of whom was a diabetic.

I've always told my folks that I hope heaven is good to them, because they've been put through the wringer in this life.

The learning curve was steep for me, and I took it in baby steps. It was hard for me as a kid to grasp something like mental illness, especially when getting me to do homework, or even something as simple as getting dressed in the morning, had become challenging tasks. It was a slow process, but even in my young mind and limited awareness, knowing *what was wrong with me* went such a long way.

Now that we knew *what* we were fighting, we could actually fight.

Things weren't improving much, but progress was being made because we finally found the right help. Shortly after discovering Dr. Abel, we were referred to a new psychiatrist, Dr. Roger Robinson in Fort Worth. In a time of such uncertainty, starting to have some pieces fall into place made a world of difference.

CHAPTER 6
2007, PART 1 – ERP

With renewed hope and a cautiously sized measurement of optimism, the end of 2006 and beginning of 2007 were a little bit better. However, my doctors told us to stay vigilant. One of the earliest things I remember learning about OCD is that there is no cure.

There is treatment, but it is… odd, to say the least.

I'll spare you the specifics of my treatment, because it got pretty strange and very extreme, but the basis of treating OCD is what is called Exposure and Response Prevention, or ERP for short.

ERP directly correlates with the definition of OCD.

The E in ERP goes with the O in OCD. You take the *obsession*, and you *expose* yourself to it.

The R in ERP goes with the C in OCD. Your *response* is your *compulsion*, and the goal of ERP is to remove that response. If you do have one – and you will because anxiety doesn't just go away – the idea of ERP is to lessen that response until it no longer interferes with your day-to-day life.

The P in ERP goes with the D in OCD. The goal is to *prevent* the *disorder*, or rather the symptoms of the disorder, which are incurable.

Did you get all that? I know, it's a lot. It was a lot for me then and it still is now, even after all these years.

I still do ERP every day. Every. Single. Day. Every moment for me is an ERP opportunity, whether I'm at work with no time to think, or at home with all the time to think. OCD is a 24/7 job – if only we got paid.

When you do ERP, you confront your obsessions. Think about someone who is afraid of rollercoasters. To get over that fear, you have two options:

1. You can avoid theme parks and never get on a ride. Or…

2. You face your fear and ride a rollercoaster. In most cases, the person ends up having fun and enjoying the ride.

With OCD, you take the thoughts that cause you anxiety, worry, distress or any feeling you *don't want to feel*, and you confront it. For me, this meant facing the things that triggered my anxiety.

For example, I would print pictures of these things, no matter how morbid. I made audio tapes reciting words, feelings and events to myself, no matter how gruesome. Or I could simply engage in a real conversation about these various obsessions. You keep going until the anxiety lowers and becomes manageable, or in the rare case, it may go away for a few seconds, perhaps even a minute.

ERP became the number one priority in my life. It also was the bane of my existence. I hated doing it. After all, who likes to face their fears?

It was difficult to begin this process, but I literally had all day. In the event I did get started, I would be minutes into a session and break down into either a fit of rage or a puddle of tears. Or both.

My most productive sessions came during my meetings with Dr. Abel. In the controlled setting of his office, I was as open with my thoughts and feelings as was possible at the time. I was still reluctant, so we turned our appointments into a game to alleviate my concerns.

Dr. Abel would ask a question, I would answer, and then he would throw a stuffed baseball toy in the air toward the couch. I'd jump through the air, catch it and then answer another question so I could keep doing my best Derek Jeter impression.

These productive sessions were hard to replicate at home. Plus, I didn't want my parents or siblings to help. The content was too weird.

I only trusted Dr. Abel and Dr. Robinson to even see the photos or hear the tapes. This made it difficult to perform ERP at home.

Even with this resistance, I started to liven up a little bit – enough that we felt reasonably confident about my seventh-grade year. My parents thought that going back to school and putting structure back in my lifestyle would be beneficial. They said I would be so happy to play school sports, a first-time opportunity in Texas public schools as a seventh grader.

I even had a girlfriend, but I only tell this story because it's an opportunity to give Colby another shoutout. This girl, who will go unnamed, dumped me the same day I asked her out. Not only that, but she also did it by writing me a note. A note that ended up on the floor of a crowded middle school hallway. But it did find its way to me because Colby picked it up off the floor, saw "To Asher" and delivered it to me.

On that… note, this isn't really the part of the book with happy endings…

By the time basketball tryouts arrived in November, something for me to feel good about, I was a lost cause. School had been a disaster from day one. I had trouble balancing my medical needs with my school obligations, and I was soon flooded by the weight of my various responsibilities.

I tried so hard to fight it off, but I was drowning.

I was miserable. Any friendships I had were all but gone, my grades were terrible, and my relationship with my parents was deteriorating. My dad and I got into shouting matches almost every night – my mom was the buffer by default – while my brother and sister kept to their own busy high school schedules, and our household became an uncomfortable, tense place.

When basketball tryouts arrived, I didn't even show. Getting out of bed in the morning had returned to the impossible endeavor it had been months prior. Whatever we were doing had worked for a little while, but I needed more help than I was getting, and more than those around me could give.

My parents and Dr. Abel decided that it was time to go back to the hospital. Now that we knew it was OCD we were dealing with, we found a hospital called The Menninger Clinic in Houston, Texas. Menninger specialized in mental illness and had a whole section of their hospital campus designated for OCD.

Once a bed became available, I was pulled out of school, and we headed for Houston.

CHAPTER 7

2007, PART 2 – MENNINGER

After limping through the final months of 2006, a spot opened at Menninger in January 2007. And it was truly a revelation. A hospital dedicated to mental illness seemed too good to be true. The OCD wing was split into adult and children's sections, and Menninger had an actual school that the OCD kids would attend while their lives took a hiatus for treatment.

The hospital was one big community, with treatment options all done privately, but everything else done together. That meant going to school with the kids from all the other sections: depression/anxiety, personality disorders, suicide prevention, trauma, addiction, bipolar disorders.

As gloomy as this life sounds, at least we did it together. We went to school, we ate at a cafeteria, we had game nights, we had outings to movies and dinners, and I humbly report that I dominated the basketball court. The counselors were impressed, and I was giddy to impress them.

I remember the friends I made at Menninger, especially Nick and Maria. Maria's cousin was a player for the Houston Rockets, and he got us locker-room passes to one of the games. I got to meet Matt Carroll, and I told him his *NBA Live* rating was 58. His teammate Melvin Ely said, "That's a bunch of bull****!" This all happened, I promise.

Even in these crazy times, I did my best to make memories. And the staff at Menninger did everything they could to give us kids some semblance of a normal life.

But, at the end of the day, we were there for treatment. Therapy took up most of the day, and it was excruciating. A kid named Steve lived across the hall from me. We hit it off on the first day when I saw him wearing his Green Lantern shirt. His type of OCD was the one most are familiar with when they think of the disease: hand-washing and cleanliness.

He would wash his hands constantly and panic when he wasn't by his room's sink. He screamed, shouted and fought – like, actually fought – his way to his bathroom so he could wash his hands. His skin was so dry and would crack and bleed easily, but this didn't stop him. He *had* to wash. It was eye-opening – the severity of this disease was not lost on me from the first moments I saw other people, especially other kids, going through the struggle.

I liked seeing him smile, and when he did find those rare moments of calm, he was a big joker. He would watch me play on my toy hoop, which made the journey from Dallas to Houston. He was either amused or bemused, depending on the day. Sometimes he even played with me, but taking advantage of those quiet, OCD-free moments was the most important thing.

If we got them.

It was an odd environment, and one that we'd find ourselves drawing attention to at the worst times. OCD never stops, so even if we weren't actively in an ERP or CBT – cognitive behavioral therapy – session, someone was always hurting. Sometimes it was me. But the constant reminders of the life my peers and I were living was humbling.

When I got there, a guy named Tony was in the kids' unit. Soon after, he graduated to the "big kids' table," but we stayed close. I've always gotten along well with people out of my age range, older and younger, and Tony was a big brother to me at Menninger. He loved basketball and played on my hoop with me until he moved to the adult wing, at which point we were no longer allowed to be in the same living area.

We still got to play together when we went to the gym, where we had many staff-and-patient basketball games. And speaking of the staff…

They were amazing. I can't think of a better word than the oft-used "amazing" to describe what these men and women did for a living. They dedicated their lives to ours. They were doctors, they were teachers, they were parents, they were mentors, and they were friends.

Dr. Thröstur Björgvinsson was the head of the operation, the director of the OCD program at Menninger which had garnered national acclaim. Mercifully, he went by "Dr. B." He personified what made the staff so effective.

When we saw him in the hallways, or the cafeteria, or anywhere on campus, he gave us the most genuine of smiles and asked how we were doing. And then asked if he could do anything for us. And then asked again about our treatment.

But if he was there at the moment *of* treatment, he didn't play any games. No moment was wasted. He pushed, and he pushed hard. He forced us to face our fears, our demons, and wouldn't let us hide from the discomfort.

Treating OCD is useless if you run, and he knew that. In the worst moments, he could seem like the devil, inflicting psychological pain on us that nobody ever wants to feel. But he did it because he cared. And he *never* stopped caring.

***

I think back on my time at Menninger and what I remember most is the staff. I remember Dr. B and his unrelenting pursuit to help every patient. I remember Reggie, who I yelled at one day for posting my ERP pictures around the rec room. I thought he was out to get me; in fact, I was certain of it on that day. He knew if he put those pictures up, I would have to either confront them or hide forever.

I remember Gelani, who would indulge me with hours of basketball talk and take me to the gym during free time. I remember

Wes, who opened the doors early on Sunday mornings so we could go on the field behind the hospital and throw the football around. I impersonated my favorite receiver, Steve Smith Sr., and provided self-commentary for Wes's throws and my catches.

I remember Nate, who kept asking me why I listened to Maroon 5 so much. Music is one of the greatest forms of therapy! Of course, he knew that – I just don't think he liked Maroon 5.

I made so much progress at Menninger, one could forgive me for thinking I had beaten OCD. At such a young age, I held on to the hope that this incurable disease *could* be beaten. Maybe I could be one in a million. Maybe.

Before I was discharged, another unusual thing happened. That's kind of the theme here, anyway.

In my final days, the staff pressed me to deal with any other fears or discomforts that I had. One immediately came to mind: I couldn't stand smoking. The action of it, the smell of it, everything about it. I find smoking absolutely revolting.

I instantly regretted sharing this information, because they had me stand by all the smokers on the hospital grounds and… just deal with it.

Deal with the smell, deal with it all. They even had me touch old cigarettes on the ground. If it sounds like torture, it's not. It felt like it at the time, but to this day, I can hold it together around smokers. I used to pull my shirt above my nose and walk in any other direction. Now, I am a *little* more discreet.

OCD is a civil war with oneself, and these are the crazy things we do to fight it.

CHAPTER 8
2008 – WINSTON

Coming home from Menninger, my first time returning from intensive treatment for OCD, was tricky. I was a lot better – I really was. But something incurable requires maintenance, and I struggled to keep up with my ERPs once I left the confines of the hospital walls.

As excited as I was to be leaving treatment, it meant starting my life again. My family and I still knew so little about OCD, although both Dr. Abel and Dr. Robinson cautioned us about the long-term reality of this disorder. Still, we couldn't help but feel like we had turned a page.

In an effort to alleviate my transition back to the world, I moved from the public school system to a private school in Dallas called The Winston School.

Winston is a K–12 school designed for kids who learn differently. That's a broad brush, but it's the truth. Students at Winston ranged from having disorders like ADD and ADHD, to full mental or physical handicaps.

Being named after Winston Churchill was probably reason enough for my history-aficionado dad to send me there, but Winston's system for "learning differently" through "non-traditional techniques" felt like a perfect match for me.

Speaking of my dad, he took on an increased workload to send me to Winston. Taking me to school went from a minute-long car ride to a 30-plus-minute trek down the Dallas North Tollway. And if you know the tollway, you know what that commute is like on a weekday morning. We found some carpoolers nearby to lessen the blow, but the circumstances were anything but ideal for my parents.

Then again, none of this is ideal. At least they got a book dedication out of it!

Everything I knew about school growing up had turned on its head. Coming from the densely populated Plano, where schools were overflowing with kids and elbow room in the hallways was a luxury, I now attended a school that instead of a thousand kids, had about a hundred.

Everything was smaller. The classes were smaller. The rooms were smaller. Even the people were smaller. The days felt shorter. But that was the whole idea. It really did help my anxiety, and rather than drowning in work and school obligations, I found enough time to take care of myself as a student and an adolescent fighting a unique battle.

The unspoken benefit of going from a big school to a small school was going from an above-average athlete to an athletic star. As an eighth grader, I played on the soccer team and the track team, and I played on the school's high school baseball team, which consisted of literally 11 players.

There were no baseball tryouts. One day during lunch, Coach Brown stood on a table and asked if anyone was interested. Ten high school kids raised their hand, and I was added later, and that was how the 2009 Winston Eagles baseball team was formed.

I couldn't play basketball as an eighth grader, and there was no middle school team, but I took over as team captain in ninth grade. Looking back, these were definitely my most memorable moments as a student athlete. It was fun to be "the guy," instead of just one of the guys, even if it was for a short time.

For all the things that changed, I did manage to have another single-day relationship in eighth grade. Not that I'm proud of it, but I finally worked up the courage to ask this girl Wylie out, just to completely chicken out and ignore her for the rest of the day.

Middle school relationships, am I right?

***

Winston was a blessing, and it allowed me to re-enter the world I used to know. There were some drawbacks, though. I had trouble making new friends, as none of my classmates lived near home in Plano. I lost touch with my public-school friends, and I spent most of my days after school doing therapy instead of hanging out with friends, going to the park or doing any "regular" kid stuff. Sports kept my mind off the loneliness, but I definitely missed the companionship of kids my age.

I tried reaching out to old friends, but we're talking about a time when the way you did this was by calling their actual house phones, installing AOL Instant Messenger or navigating the mysterious cyber ways of Myspace.

Instead, I focused on my love of sports, my growing passion for movies and my interest in reading. I read all the books from the *A Series of Unfortunate Events* collection, and I was hooked on the John Feinstein young adult sports mysteries.

As a sports lover, I had played in fantasy leagues for as long as I could remember. In 2008, I decided to start my own league. Struggling to branch out, I looked inward and realized that I had built a community of close friends online.

We've all heard the horror stories about online relationships, but some of my best friends, and most of the future members of my fantasy baseball and basketball leagues, came from online forums and websites.

Specifically, I met two gents named Shawn and Miguel on the question-and-answer website Yahoo! Answers. As crazy as it sounds, these guys became two of my best friends, and we still keep in touch today. Both of them have been long-time members of my fantasy leagues since way back in 2008. Our baseball league is still active today – the basketball league folded due to my dwindling interest in the NBA – but truly, I'm grateful and proud of what those leagues did for me and the people I met through them.

All in all, perhaps through unusual means, my life actually started to feel like something other people were doing.

After being introduced to the OCD community at Menninger in 2007, my parents and I attended the International OCD Foundation Conference for three years in a row. The first one happened to take place right in Houston. A summer later in 2008, we went to Minnesota. In 2009, we went to Boston.

Maybe it's my instinctive gift to wrap my childhood memories in bliss, but those summer conferences were good times. Learning about the thing that you live with all day, every day, all the time, is not just enlightening but extremely reassuring. Spending a weekend with other people, mostly kids, who also fought this same uphill battle, reminded me of my time at Menninger.

We talked – casually – about our obsessions, our compulsions, our symptoms, our tics, our day-to-day struggles… and none of it was awkward. All of us were so used to living our lives in our own, weird way. Sharing this experience made me feel like an actual human being, and that felt great.

Through all this time, I kept my life in check, even if it was a delicate balance.

Every day was a struggle, but it was a struggle I could manage. I continued seeing Dr. Abel twice a week, Dr. Robinson every few months, and I did ERP three times a day, sometimes more if I was either doing so well that I felt confident, or I was going through a tough spot and needed the additional help.

The problem with OCD, or any incurable disease, is that you can only do your best with what you have. I had ERP, I had my parents, I had my doctors. But I still had OCD. And it wasn't going anywhere. In the back of my mind, I held onto the hope that one day it would go away, or even be surgically removed. But I also knew – and feared – that this would be my life forever.

Every moment of my day was held in place by that thought. I'm not sure if it kept me grounded, kept me on guard or both. Probably both, but it unsettled me all the same. My life started to look and feel more normal on the outside, and I put on quite the front at home so my parents and siblings wouldn't worry. I desperately wanted them to believe that *I was better*. And that *the treatment worked*.

Both those things were true, but I sweated through car rides and family meals without getting stuck or performing compulsion rituals just so they would think everything was okay.

But how ERP therapy works is not unlike how we deal with emotions: You can't bottle up your feelings, nor can you bottle up your obsessions and compulsions. If you do, the impending explosion will have consequences. Eventually, my luck ran out, and I started to get stuck more. And more. And more.

But I was still functioning, so we made each day work as best we could and hoped for the future. My medication would increase, then decrease a little, then go back up. Each day presented the same circumstances, but there were always different challenges and different methods to get me from waking up in the morning to finally going back to bed at night.

CHAPTER 9

2009 – BOULEVARD OF BELIEVABLE DREAMS

With my life and health being managed with a delicate but somehow efficient balance, I got my first job in January 2009. My dream as a kid, like so many, was to play professional sports. I wanted to play professional baseball or basketball in the MLB or NBA, and before I got sick three years earlier, I spent every waking moment working on my game.

I learned early on that even if I had a clean bill of health from the start, being a professional athlete was a long shot for a Jewish kid who would be fortunate to surpass 5 foot 7. I remember early in my life, in the middle of one of my hours-long practice sessions on our home basketball hoop, my dad gritted his teeth and gave me "the talk."

"It's 8:30," he said. "It's time for dinner."

"Please, just five more minutes," I pleaded. "Just one more shot."

"Practice all you want, but you're not going to play in the NBA."

Hard words for a fifth grader to hear, but my dad has never been one to shy away from the truth. I respect that. At 11, I respected it less. But really, I respect it.

Like many of the Jewish faith, I switched my focus from playing the game to working in the game. I wanted to be a sports journalist, a dream that would mutate over time into sports broadcasting, but as a young kid, I had a true passion for writing.

In an effort to break into the sports world, I got a job as a batboy with the Frisco RoughRiders, the Double-A Minor League Baseball affiliate of the Texas Rangers. As a family, we were season ticket holders of the Rangers, Mavericks and, since their inception in 2003, the RoughRiders.

I spent many nights at the ballpark as a kid, chasing autographs pregame and running after foul balls during the game. After the final out, while people chased dirty baseballs or asked minor leaguers for their bats, which the players literally had to pay for themselves, I'd find a coach and add to my collection of lineup cards.

It made perfect sense to try and get a job there, and I had an in with a family we knew, the Bodzins. David, their son who was a few years older than me, had been a batboy for the RoughRiders before going to work in a similar position with the Rangers. His parents, the wonderful Mark and Sandy, were regulars at Dr. Pepper Ballpark in Frisco. Though Mark didn't work for the team, he knew everyone in the front office on a first-name basis.

Working for a Minor League Baseball team was an eye-opening experience for so many reasons. I could write a book alone on the stories I have working in the sports industry, particularly at the minor league levels of the MLB and NBA.

My first day with the RoughRiders still sticks out in my memory. It was a preseason exhibition game between the Rangers and the Kansas City Royals. What I remember most, outside of leaving school early, has nothing to do with baseball.

When the Royals arrived at the park, veteran relief pitcher Kyle Farnsworth had a big, big problem: He forgot his PSP on the team bus. That's a PlayStation Portable, for those born before 1990 or after 2005.

That bus was due to leave any minute, and they sent me sprinting after it. I made it, retrieved his PSP and brought it back to him feeling like an absolute hero.

Later, during the game, I went back into the locker room to retrieve more baseballs, and he was in there playing on the gaming device.

Side note: MLB relief pitchers have an important job, but when they aren't in the game or getting ready to go in the game – *especially* for an exhibition matchup – there really isn't a lot to do. So, he was just chilling. And he had his video game, thanks to me!

Another thing I remember from that day was my brief interaction with Royals superstar pitcher Zack Greinke. Greinke is famous for his talent as a pitcher, but also because he was diagnosed with a social anxiety disorder in 2006, three years earlier.

My disorder was a private matter, but his celebrity status didn't afford him such a luxury. Obviously, I did not bring it up to him – not on my first day, much less as a 15-year-old. On top of that was the most important point: It wasn't any of my business. But to see someone with a mental illness, up close, who had achieved incredible success with his life, was pretty cool.

In that season, he would go on to make his first All-Star appearance. Six years later, the Arizona Diamondbacks signed him to a six-year, $206.5 million contract. I would say he's done pretty well for himself, which is certainly an accomplishment for the unseen mental illness community.

***

The most influential event of my life during my breakthrough baseball job had nothing to do with baseball. The pitching coach for the RoughRiders was Jeff Andrews. Andrews had two sons, one of them an 8-year-old named Alex. I've never had a younger sibling, and my older brother and I have had starkly different interests for as long as I remember. Alex, to reference the classic *Austin Powers* trilogy, was my Mini-Me.

His life revolved around baseball, as did most of mine, and I found in him a little brother that I never had. To this day, he is still my little bro.

He lives in Oklahoma, so we talk from a distance, but we talk all the time. We talk about baseball, we talk about our beloved *MLB The Show* baseball video game, and my relationship with him is one of my most cherished. I love him like a brother and think of him as one, as well as a friend.

I've always thought the world of kids and had an unusually high patience and/or tolerance for their craziness. In eighth grade, I had a free period, and I had the opportunity to help the kindergarten teacher with her class. The unshakable hope and wonder present in a child is a popular cliche, but cliches are repeated for a reason.

But back to the RoughRiders – when their games were over, and I had finished cleaning out the dugout and bullpen, and the water coolers were filled for the next day's batting practice, I took Alex off his dad's hands when he had his post-game coaches meeting.

I took Alex to the pool in right field of Dr. Pepper Ballpark, and we threw a ball back and forth while reciting every team's roster in Major League Baseball. I would quiz him on the most random of players – and he would get them all right.

"Shortstop for the Pittsburgh Pirates," I would ask before throwing the baseball in the air as he jumped into the water.

In between his leap and hitting the water, he would shout, "Jack Wilson!"

This cycle of names went for about 30 minutes after most home games. I had a hole in my life for companionship, finding it difficult to make friends and butting heads with my family members. But in Alex, I found something that brought me a lot of joy and added another reason among many to look forward to this job I was so fortunate to have at a young age.

I spent just about every night that summer at the ballpark. They were good times with the players, with Alex, and just spending so much time around the game of baseball. At this point in that job, batboys were allowed to shag batting practice with the players. I showed up to work well before it was time to clock in time just to do this.

It was a blast. And I'm fairly confident the players enjoyed having me out there. In particular, I remember sharing the pregame Texas heat with former RoughRiders like Mitch Moreland and Tim Smith. Moreland, of course, went on to the big leagues and won a World Series with the Boston Red Sox in 2018.

One time, pitcher C.J. Wilson was on an injury rehabilitation assignment in Frisco, and I snagged a flyball headed straight at him while he was on his pregame jog. Not to take credit for the $77.5 million contract he signed two years later, but you're welcome, C.J.!

With my first job, I also got a taste of the working world, for better and worse. This was a highly sought-after job for kids, and several of the batboy positions had gone to friends of family within the organization, regardless of their qualifications or even interest.

This resulted in me butting heads with a few of the other batboys, begrudging my way into daily arguments about their lack of responsibility and desire to milk the position for all the perks and none of the work. But again – it was mostly good times.

When my ninth-grade year came to a close, my overall health was in a decent enough spot that my parents and doctors granted my request to return to public school. There was hesitation and caution, but it was something I badly wanted and for which I really fought.

As helpful as private school was, I felt alone and left out from people my age. Winston had done wonders for me and set my life on a manageable course. However, the private school presented a life that was exactly that: private.

I had little connection with other kids and tried desperately to establish friendships through websites like Facebook or over text. I can tell you now what a bad idea that is, but at the time I just wanted *something*. To feel like I belonged. Anywhere. At all.

Returning to public school meant being exposed to the social climate I once knew. It also meant removing the safety nets that Winston provided. The chance was one I was willing to take, more so than my parents, who questioned if I was ready. But despite advancements on the OCD front, I began to feel depressed and ostracized from kids my age. I wanted to go back.

***

As soon as tenth grade started, I fell apart.

I was instantly overwhelmed by, well, everything. I no longer had a system constructed to guide me, I couldn't handle the workload, and I wasn't equipped to enter a high school social hierarchy I had never known. My old friends had new friends, and through it all, I didn't have any time to spend on myself.

At Winston, my schedule was built to include breaks during school, and I had found the balance to have time for ERP after school. My life was reliant on structure, and I didn't recognize just how important that was. That, or I was simply too determined to get back to the life I had before my diagnosis almost four years earlier.

Now, that structure had all fallen apart. To be clear, it's not like I was ever symptom-, worry- or OCD-free at any point. But I hoped to keep it together enough to get back into the world I'd once spent every day in without a second thought.

Or third thought. Or fourth. Or the non-stop wave of thoughts from which I never got a break.

My obsessions became stronger. My compulsions became more frequent. My repetitive tics got out of control. I used to repeat tasks to try and get the feeling "just right." Then, that feeling of "just right" had to be achieved twice. Sometimes three times. Four. Five.

Hours would pass by, and by the time I broke the ritual chain, I was drenched in sweat and fully exhausted. Most of the time, the relief lasted just minutes. Then it began again, and I was stuck all over. I was trading hours of suffering for minutes of freedom, and I was getting ripped off.

Whole days were lost, and I was soon designated as a special education student to give me some of that needed structure and help. To the school's credit, they had what was called the BASE program. It wasn't strictly special education (SPED), but an extension of the system where kids with anxiety or depression, or social, reading, writing and other types of limitations, could get help they needed.

This included me, but my entrance into the SPED program all but destroyed my chance to reconnect with old friends – not that it was going well anyway. I now spent most of my time in BASE – if I even mustered up the courage to go to school that day – and spent almost no time in actual classrooms.

My problems got as bad as they had ever been. My home life shattered. My relationship with my family crumbled.

***

My mom is a doctor, and her work schedule is basically 24/7. Anyone who knows her or our family can tell you that "24/7" isn't really hyperbole. So, her schedule left my dad as my primary caretaker – and boy, did I put him through hell.

When the relapse began, my medication was increased to try and combat the storm. I was on so much medication that I could not get myself up in the middle of the night if I needed the bathroom. That meant, at 16 years old, I was a bedwetter.

I was so drugged that I didn't even realize it happened, and my dad had to forcibly usher me into a morning shower, and then I would get stuck in there. There was so much yelling between him and me, and while it was all well-intentioned from his end, it exacerbated the struggle, and the divide between my dad and I continued to grow.

Rarely did a day not include multiple shouting matches. In 2009 and 2010, I think I aged my dad a century. On many days, I was so immobile and so broken that we just gave up on school. Phone calls were made to the school front office, and I just went back to bed.

A bleak motto of mine became, "If I'm sleeping, I'm not thinking." I would sleep as much as possible, just to avoid any conscious brain activity. Sadly, my unconscious sleep was not immune to my demons, though it was miles better than being awake.

My relationship with my dad and family got so strained that I wouldn't even stay home. I spent a lot of days at my aunt and uncle's house just down the street. My dad's sister Debbie Rabinowitz lived minutes away and mostly worked from home.

Debbie took me off my dad's hands to give him a break. I did the same amount of nothingness under a different roof just to give my dad a reprieve. After all, he had an actual life to live and a job to work on top of his full-time, unpaid duty as my caretaker.

Around this time, Debbie's oldest son – my cousin Marcus – got a dog. Debbie and my Uncle Fred were primarily in charge of Miley, the sweetest little puppy, and she became my de facto therapy dog. I spent as much time with Miley as possible, and she slept with me after I started spending more days and nights at the "Binos'," as we called the Rabinowitz household.

Their youngest son Harris is ten months younger than me and was also a classmate of mine. Harris was then and still is now one of the most selfless, caring people I will ever know. He was popular at school, and he used his status to keep an eye on me. Ironically, some of his best friends were my old best friends from elementary school.

I had bullies. People pick on the kids who have, let's say, differences – those who can't defend themselves. But nobody picked on me with Harris around. He also would check on me in the hallways, which went a long way.

On the days I managed to go to school, it wasn't pretty. I wanted so badly to be in class and try to appear normal to my teachers and classmates. But the obsessions and compulsions were too distracting. If I wasn't self-conscious about people watching me and my tics, they were still too disruptive to justify keeping me in a normal classroom environment.

I somehow managed to play on the tenth grade basketball team, but I think my friend T.J. put in some sort of good word. That, or the potential I had shown coming up in the Plano system, and my performance in private school, had lent me some credibility.

Being on the basketball team was the saving grace of my tenth grade school year. My experience as a player was not good. I missed a lot of practices for the aforementioned reasons, and I didn't get along with my coach. None of us did.

When a coach asks what he's doing wrong, he means it rhetorically. Before one of our usual practices that was all running and no basketball, we decided as players in the locker room to take a stand. Well, it turns out, when the chips are down, tenth grade athletes don't *really* want to start a mutiny.

So, I ended up on that island alone, with a suspension to show for talking back. Despite this instance, I made some incredible memories with the guys on that team. If anything, we bonded together over the challenges we faced from our lack of leadership.

Jake, of fifth grade *Star Wars* birthday party fame, was on the team. Colby, too. Then, there was Qualen, who gave us stories to cherish and memories to hold onto that are not even remotely appropriate to put in these pages.

During one of the games, when I was in my usual spot in the doghouse, the coach asked who wanted to play, and Qualen volunteered me. That comment didn't go over well, and we got suspended together. I'm not condoning these actions, but Qualen and I did everything together that year, for better or… honestly, still better.

While my friends on the team brought moments of joy and escape, on a personal level, I continued to implode. I did everything I could to hold it together during basketball, because that was something that felt normal.

I was doing something that I probably would have been doing in my personal alternate reality – my life without OCD. But the air popped from the balloon once I went home.

***

Every year during winter break, my family and the Rabinowitz family take a trip. Almost always, we go to Mexico. But in 2009, the plan was an exciting trip all over Europe.

However, for my dad and me, it was back to Houston.

CHAPTER 10

WINTER BREAK 2009 – HOUSTON OCD PROGRAM

My mom's non-stop work schedule earned her priority to go overseas. That left my dad to make the trip with me to Houston, where we rented an apartment to call our temporary home. He and my mom switched out mid-trip, but these repeated ventures to Houston would pretty much be my dad and me in the future, cooped up together, which added cracks to our already fracturing relationship.

As I've said, he's not much of a feeler, so trying to get compassion from him proved a tough task. He's one of the nicest, most charitable, generous people I know, but showing l-o-v-e has never come easy for him.

When I was really young, every night before bed, I would run to four corners of the house where my mom, dad, brother and sister were all doing whatever it was they were doing. Always a creature of habit, part of my nighttime routine was telling each family member I loved them. The answers went something like this:

Mom: "Love you too, sweetie. Have a good day tomorrow."

Brother: "You too, Cuna," my family nickname from *The Lion King* since year one of my life.

Sister: "I love… cake," a reference to our favorite TV show, *That '70s Show*.

Dad: "Okay. See you in the morning."

Like I said: My dad is a wonderful human being. A lot of men aren't very open with their feelings. I have no ill will at all toward him for this. I'm just stating the facts.

***

In late 2009, my life had re-entered its own hell and had gotten so bad, again, that hospitalization once again had to be the answer.

If you will refer to your earlier reading, I said in Chapter 7 that "a hospital dedicated to mental illness seemed too good to be true." Well, since my trip to Menninger in 2007, the OCD wing at the hospital had lost funding. This happened in December 2008. It had indeed turned out to be too good to be true.

Fortunately, the OCD staff at Menninger would not give up on their mission. They found a large, multi-purpose home in the city of Houston to continue their important work and moved there in February 2009.

This is where I was headed in December 2009. At 16, I was still too young for inpatient treatment, so my dad and I stayed together, and he drove me to the Houston OCD "clinic" (the house) every morning and picked me up every afternoon.

When he traded out to go on the family trip, my mom took over. Their sacrifice did not register with me then, but soon after, it hit. And it hurt. To take them away from an international super-trip to Europe with the rest of the extended family? That sucked. They never mentioned it once and have never uttered a word of inconvenience in relation to my OCD, but keeping them from a good time like that does sting.

It was incredibly odd to see the same staff members I had left two and a half years earlier with such high hopes. I had grown a lot physically, but mentally I had almost seemed to regress. I was losing out on key developmental years of my life, and the effects were showing.

Before we traveled to Houston, the staff made their medical inquiries to prepare for round two of my treatment in the program. Of the things they asked, they really wanted to know what I did in my free time.

How did I "escape"?

The answers were pretty simple: sports and video games. And that was what they wanted to know to revolutionize my treatment.

They told me to bring my PlayStation 3, and they were going to build me up to where I could do ERP while also doing something I enjoyed. The idea was that combining pleasure with your triggers could help you find a happy balance.

As ridiculous as it sounds – kind of the moral of the story here anyway – it worked.

Once it did, the next thing was walking to the nearby park to shoot baskets. The catch: I had to bring my ERP tools. In this instance, this was my looped tape recordings that recited my obsessions in graphic form. Wherever I went, it came with me.

It was hard. Honestly, I was pissed off by my treatment. It felt like they were stealing my hobbies from me by pairing them with the things I tried so hard to avoid. Those thoughts and feelings that caused me anxiety and pain were now being mixed with the few activities I could do to find peace.

It felt like some sort of twisted torture, just like they had done at Menninger. And again, I was proven wrong. They were right, and during the two weeks I was there during my winter break, I *did* get better.

Two weeks was all we had, because I needed to be back in school. But it was a very productive two weeks, and I came home with renewed confidence.

***

During this short time, and with the staff's help, I also had an important self-realization. Another form of therapy they encouraged me to do was meditation. I had a hard time shutting down my mind, so they met me in the middle and proposed a compromise.

"What about music?"

I started listening to music every day. My favorite artists from years past were scattered in my memory bank, but thanks to this new thing called YouTube, their music was now all there for the taking. I found comfort in the music of bands like Maroon 5, Green Day, The Killers and The All-American Rejects, and my childhood fandom of *NSYNC resurfaced.

*NSYNC was my first concert, with my mom, in 2002. I listened to Justin Bieber's early stuff and maintain to this day that it is his best work. I got lost in an endless library of music, which proved to be an effective and enduring form of therapy.

And then I went home. There was reason for optimism, but the reality was I had spent just two weeks in the controlled environment of treatment. I made a promise to myself to recommit to ERPs and my mental health. Unfortunately, if promises were crackers, we'd all be fat. That promise was made by a very immature teenager with little life experience.

When I got home, we tried to live a normal life again. My parents wanted to send me to driver's ed, with the hope that I would get my license by the time I was 17 – a year late, but a win, all things considered. I actually powered through that somehow, utilizing a window of post-treatment bliss to get my license in the winter of 2010. I didn't start driving, but I had the credentials. It was something.

I did my best to hang in there, and basketball was a big help. Through basketball, I spent more time with friends. Jake and I went to the NBA All-Star Rookie-Sophomore Game, which was in Dallas that year. We recognized NBA player Jonas Jerebko getting into a cab after the game, somehow completely missing 2009 Rookie of the Year Tyreke Evans.

My friendship with T.J. grew, too, and his mom hosted an All-Star party and invited the entire school basketball team. We also turned the construction lot across his house into a wiffle ball field. And, of course, there was Qualen and the wacky adventures we went on every day during school and basketball practice.

There were moments of triumph, but ultimately, it was a Band-Aid on a broken leg. The cracks started to spread, and the punches I'd previously dodged or at least defended started to land. By the time my tenth grade year was winding down, we had already made plans to return to Houston.

CHAPTER 11

SUMMER 2010 – BACK TO HOUSTON

I felt a lot of things when I returned to the Houston OCD Program. Mostly, I felt disappointed. But I also felt scared, I felt angry, I felt sad, I was depressed, and everything seemed hopeless.

And I really felt like I was letting people down.

My OCD – and, therefore, my life – felt so out of my control, but I also recognized that it still was *my* life. And *my* OCD. I just could not figure out a way to get past the crippling anxiety. Every thought I had caused me so much stress, and then distress, and the compulsions – or rituals – were getting as bad as they had ever been.

More time than ever was spent on my tics. There would be moments where I would just tap, tap, tap, tap, tap on a desk or object or even my dad's incredibly annoyed shoulder. I would tap for minutes on end, sometimes hours, until my mind felt like it could move on.

Another thing I felt was very, very tired. I spent most of my waking hours stuck. When I wasn't stuck, I was so worried about *not getting stuck*, that I might as well have been stuck. Quality of life was not good. Life just wasn't good.

At a particularly low moment, I threatened to use a kitchen knife on myself. I had no intention, nor have I ever had any intention of ending my life or giving in to my OCD, but there have been times where I at least entertained the notion. They are the darkest of memories, and it hurts to even know I came so close, but they were also moments that triggered wake-up calls in an already sleepless life.

One of those low moments came right before we went back to Houston in the summer of 2010. I was distraught about having to go back, caught between not wanting to go into treatment for a third time and asking myself what the point of it all was.

There was no cure. It was never going to go away. Maybe this was just my lot in life. "It could be worse," I would tell myself. I could have cancer or an intellectual or physical disability. Maybe living with OCD was just what I was meant to do.

That kind of defeatist talk got me nowhere fast, so back in Houston we were.

When I got to Houston, the doctors asked me something point-blank that I had been avoiding admitting for some time.

"How honest are you with your ERPs?"

The truth was that I did them. I did them every day. But I cheated my way through the hardest moments. I was putting in the time, but not my best work. The truth was I didn't want to do it. I did do it, but only halfway.

I didn't want to face my deepest fears and obsessions, so I focused on conquering the things that still triggered me but weren't at the top of my list of obsessions.

Now, I know this all sounds very vague. But I cannot get specific about what my biggest triggers were. I can't do that because they were people. They still are in the present day.

My obsessions stemmed from things that have to do with people: the way they looked, the way they acted, the way they were. To name them would be inappropriate and wouldn't do much but make this personal, which is not the goal of me telling my story.

Let's talk more about anxiety. Nobody likes to have it. It makes them feel uncomfortable, and nobody likes to feel out of their comfort zone. The thing is, when someone has anxiety, they deal with it. This usually happens on a subconscious level. On a conscious level, perhaps they give themselves a little pep talk or change their activity. But usually, anxiety dissipates without giving it a literal thought.

For someone with OCD, or any anxiety disorder, that just isn't enough. The anxiety is literally crippling. It's paralyzing, and we can't move on until it's gone – we can't do *anything* until it's gone.

And a mental disorder is a living thing, so the more attention and time it gets, the bigger it gets. That is what happens to anxiety when we give it power – it gets worse and worse.

Instead of the anxiety temporarily increasing, then coming down and finally going away, people with mental illnesses like OCD cannot justify that curve. Anxiety for us increases and increases and keeps growing. That's the obsession.

Rather than coping or using life skills that humans use every day to combat unwanted emotions, I would undergo my compulsions, like tics and rituals, to alleviate the anxiety. This works in theory, but it is time-consuming and debilitating, and even when my anxiety would finally drop, it still ended up in a higher place than it started before the initial decrease.

For a visual reference, picture a bell curve that never returns to equilibrium. The cycle continues to repeat itself, with the anxiety's highest point continuing to heighten over time.

When I cheated myself on ERPs, my anxiety continued to grow. If it came down, it came down in increments, rather than returning to a baseline, which is the point of therapies like ERP and CBT.

So, when the doctors asked me to be honest about my ERPs, I did what most scared teenagers would do: I lied.

At this pivotal moment in the summer of 2010, I didn't just cheat myself. I cheated my doctors, I cheated my family, I definitely cheated my family's wallets, and I cheated everyone's time, everyone's efforts in helping me.

I was so afraid of facing my true fears that I simply chose to keep half-assing my treatment. I continued to leave treatment in a slightly better spot than before, but never returned home at the place I needed to be, the place I *could* be, the place the Houston OCD Program staff intended for me to be, the place my family desperately hoped for me to be, or the place I was telling everyone that I was now in after getting help yet again.

If this sounds like reckless, careless, ignorant behavior… it is. Sure, I can use the "sick, terrified teenage boy" excuse, and truthfully, I will use it, but by refusing to truly face my worst obsessions, I was doing a disservice to myself, my family and the best help money could buy.

I just… I couldn't. My worst obsessions caused levels of anxiety that I literally could not handle. I would bite my nails until my fingers crawled with blood, twist my hair in knots until I was balding, tear apart furniture… I couldn't take it. I would do *anything* to not feel that pain. And lying about it is one of my biggest regrets.

***

When I was a kid, my mind was always racing. This resulted in a lot of self-micromanagement, and it drove me a little mad. I've always been a very nervous person, a quality I inherited from my mother without question. Nerves will do you some good, as they have served her in the ways of being the ultimate caregiver; a very protective, caring parent; and a loving, hands-on, involved person.

But nerves will also make you, let's say, uptight, on edge and very, very restless. That's her, and that's me. For me, this manifested in ADD, ADHD and eventually OCD, an anxiety disorder and the whole shebang. For her, it means 24 hours and 7 days of work and being all things to all people at all times.

When I was young, I was notorious for being fidgety and, wouldn't you know it, extremely compulsive. I picked the fuzz off my blankets, depositing the balls of cloth behind my bed, which would require a routine clean-up from our housekeeper Carmen, who is basically my second mom. The amount of blanket residue would form basketball-sized furballs.

These habits have persisted to this day, despite my improvements. There's no better proof than two areas: my first car's steering wheel, and the wall behind the couch in my family's game room.

The steering wheel had been peeled off and picked apart, a way for me to let off some of the many different emotions I felt while I drove. The wall behind the game-room couch had been scratched away, repaired and then scratched again. The upstairs TV room at my parent's house is basically my second bedroom – it's literally where I'm typing these words now.

It's the room in which I spent the most time in my entire life, and it's consequentially the room that I've had the most trouble in. It is, in fact, the room where I remember my very first symptom while I was playing *NBA Live* way back in 2006.

When anyone gets nervous, they tend to look for things to do with their hands. I did that when I *wasn't* nervous, so when I was indeed feeling anxious, I would pick my nails, my hair, blankets, the walls – anything I could reach.

But the coup de grâce of irresponsible behavior came in the summer of 2010, when I threw a tantrum to get out of treatment a little early so I could come home and play in my rec baseball team's championship. Of course, I loved baseball, but I had missed most of the season because of treatment, and my discharge date was coming anyway. I barely even got to work my RoughRiders job in 2010. So, we left a little early to get back in time for the championship game.

Which we lost. And I wasted a whole summer – and everyone's time, too.

CHAPTER 12

SCHOOL 2010–2011 – JUNIOR YEAR

Coming home from treatment, I had everyone on pins and needles. They didn't know that I had compromised my time in Houston, and even though I did, I still did get some good work done. I came back improved, and from the outside looking in, everyone was a lot more hopeful than I was. Quicker than ever, and more transparently than ever, things unraveled yet again.

In Texas, the school system kind of does its own thing – that's Texas for ya. High school is broken into two parts, with junior high consisting of ninth and tenth grade, which I had just completed at Winston in ninth grade and Shepton in tenth grade. Part two would be senior high school, 11th and 12th grade, which I would attend just down the street from our house at Plano West.

It was now time to enter senior high school, and for a myriad of reasons, it was too much for me. At the onset of the school year, every day was spent in BASE. I also started to miss a lot more school. In fact, more than ever.

Looking back, I'm not even sure how I got high school credits. Perhaps it's because, as my therapist put it recently during one of our monthly phone calls, I would *do the work*, it would just take forever to get it done, between all my constant self-interruptions and the heavy workload of an upperclassman.

In all the chaos, my parents and I decided to give driving another shot, more out of necessity than capability. My brother's hand-me-down Ford Explorer was there for the taking, but I wasn't ready to be behind the wheel of a car. Still, that was a priority for me, and I ended up continuing my driver's education career at a virtual driving instruction place somewhere in the area.

I hardly remember much of it, just that it was extremely helpful, and more people should do it. I also remember that you could actually kill civilians in the simulation, which is pretty dark. It was like playing a video game, except instead of racing through downtown Los Angeles, you're stopping at red lights, checking your mirrors and staying under the speed limit in your local neighborhood.

Soon enough, I started to drive. For as bad as my OCD always was, when I was driving a car, or heck, even five years earlier at my Bar Mitzvah when I avoided the throat tics during my Torah reading, I had the fight-or-flight ability to keep it together when there was simply no other option.

There were some notable hiccups. While driving with my mom, I turned left into oncoming traffic at an intersection. We quickly got out and swapped places at a red light so she could get in the driver's seat, and she steered us out of harm's way.

Another time, again at an intersection on my way to school, my then-ritual tic was flashing my high beams to "reset" my thoughts. Unbeknownst to me, there was a car across the way – a police car. Thankfully, for whatever reason, he didn't pull me over or pay it any mind, and I avoided an uncomfortable and confusing altercation.

For the most part, I held it together behind the wheel. As bad as my mental health was, my human instincts for safety prevailed when I was driving a car.

The moments after driving were, therefore, excruciating. Once I parked, whether in the school parking lot, at home or at work, I was always stuck. But I kept it together on the road, which is the least you can ask any driver to do.

The downside of having a car was that I became responsible for getting myself to school. I had trouble enough making it to school, and when I did, I spent all my time in BASE anyway. So, for a lot of days, I just stopped going. Sometimes I went, came home for lunch, and then got so stuck that by the time I got out of a trance, it was 2pm, and the school day was lost.

Life continued to be a miserable existence. I tried as best I could to get to school, see my classmates and try to make friends, or simply get out of the house. The reality was I was never in class, and I tried to make friends through my BlackBerry phone. (Remember those?!)

It was detached, it was impersonal, and truthfully, I was stalking people on social media to try and make some sort of connection.

My school friendships went from few to none. The close friends I had managed to keep around started to see me less and less – not because of them, but because of me. I was never leaving the house, and we were all confused, emotionally challenged high schoolers at the time. I didn't have the mental capacity to tell them what was wrong, and if they asked, I don't even think I would have been honest.

My friends at the time were the members of my fantasy sports leagues, specifically Shawn and Miguel, to whom I still talk to this day. I consider them great friends, but no matter how great our sports conversations were, both guys were still thousands of miles away.

Hindsight is an obvious benefit (and would be a sweet superpower), but I handled my friends leaving me very, very poorly. The lonelier I became, the more combative and argumentative I got.

As I became further estranged from my friends, compounded with the fact that I was in a special education program, I began to pick up more bullies in my later years of school. They stuck to the bully basics, calling my peers and me the R-word and challenging my former friends to take a side, something that only made me angrier and more resentful.

For a select low few, the Jew jokes were there as well, as they had been all my life. The K-word was used as people pleased, and some even threw coins on floors and encouraged me to go pick them up (which I did so I could have lunch money).

Fortunately, part of being a Jew is having an impenetrable sense of humor. I don't know why that is, but I thank Adam Sandler anyway. I handled my bullies with witty comebacks and quick retorts. That only made them angrier – and the situation worse – and put my old friends in even more uncomfortable spots, but that was how I handled it, for better or for worse.

In my mind, my warped mind, I already dealt with so much on the inside that I wasn't going to take anything on the outside. Just "letting it go" wasn't in my behavioral capacity, and I made things worse to the point of receiving death threats.

High school is a crazy place, and this was a pretty specific time for rising behavioral issues in the upper-class community I lived in.

***

My medication continued to increase, and consequently my appetite did as well. I started to eat multiple lunches a day, one of them usually coming from the dollar menu at McDonald's. I woke up restless in the middle of the night and had microwavable pizzas from the kitchen freezer in those early morning hours.

I was always hungry and always eating. I'd been fit my whole life, raised in a household that ate healthy foods, and I was always active. My siblings and I joke now that dinner was either grilled chicken or salmon, depending on the night of the week. But now, my meals were double. I was putting on weight. And fast. This made me even more depressed and hateful of myself, and the loneliness persisted.

The OCD was bad, but now I was too out of shape to even continue my out-of-school basketball and baseball teams. Everything I managed to hold on to in life started slipping away.

I did manage to maintain one extracurricular activity: the school newspaper. I still loved sports and had the same dream to become a journalist in the industry. In the spring of 2011, I was chosen amongst hundreds of finalists in the Dallas-Ft. Worth area to be a contributor in the "Student Voices" section of the *Dallas Morning News*.

I wrote about the life of a batboy, and my submission was chosen to be published in the actual newspaper. It was a pretty big win for my confidence, and my folks were damn proud, which made me happy.

It's fun to be happy, and there was sadly a short supply of that feeling for the Feltmans. As the year dragged on, going back to the hospital was inevitable. However, I was going to be 18 at the end of May, which meant I could now be an inpatient at a medical facility.

Having tried Houston three times – and it seeming ineffective because of my own fears and shortcomings – and considering the fact that I could now stay in a hospital without parent supervision, we looked elsewhere and found out about the McLean Hospital in Boston, Massachusetts.

CHAPTER 13
SUMMER 2011 – MCLEAN

Like Menninger, McLean was a renowned psychiatric hospital. The difference since December 2008 was that McLean still had an OCD wing. I left right after the last day of 11th grade – just before my birthday – but because I was turning 18 in mere days, I was able to get a spot as an inpatient at McLean.

Immediately, the environment was different. Where Menninger could feel like a summer camp at times, McLean was very strict. I was in an environment of only adults, even if some of them were young adults like myself. Staff were not there to be friendly and build relationships, but to treat you and clock out.

For better or mostly worse, you were always seen as a patient only.

Some days, it felt like a prison. In Houston, I got homesick a lot. In Boston, I was homesick all the time. Sure, I was way across the country now, instead of across the state, but McLean tended to lack a homey feeling that the staff at Houston seemed to go out of their way to provide.

Perhaps my earliest memory at McLean involves a fellow patient named Bruce, who also had irritable bowel syndrome, which meant most of our conversations took place stall to stall early in the mornings. He warned me in a rather cryptic, paranoid way that McLean has a long waiting list, and their best way to get patients in and out was to discharge you at the first moment they thought you were ready.

Things at McLean always seemed to be on edge. Not because of Bruce's prophecy, but there was almost a weird patients-versus-staff culture. That isn't to say I didn't bond with some staff members, but I can't remember anyone's name. On the other hand, I can still list off Houston employees without trouble.

On the plus side, I got along great with the other patients. That mutual understanding and unspoken bond – sharing something that only *we* could understand – brought us together. I got a lot of good work done in the group therapy sessions.

To make up for my mistakes in Houston, I committed myself more than ever to ERP. I was making progress again but missing the love and support from the staff. I got my motivation from fellow patients, such as Peter, an older gentleman who I always ended up partnering with on our group outings.

One day at a mall in Boston, I even worked up the courage to talk to a girl thanks to Peter's prodding and Ben Kenobi-like wisdom.

"I'm actually not from here," she said.

"Oh, me neither!" I replied.

And that's all I remember. But I did it! And Peter was proud.

I hit it off with my first neighbor, Natasha, a 70-year-old woman who was getting OCD treatment for the first time in her life. That put things in perspective for me, as many things did, and intensified my commitment to getting better. I vividly remember introducing her to Maroon 5's music and still get a kick out of picturing her dancing to "Moves Like Jagger," which I had recently discovered by watching season one of *The Voice*.

(That's right, Dad. I was watching your favorite show *before* you. You're welcome.)

There was Clark, the only other kid my age, and while we had little in common, we nevertheless bonded over the circumstances. He was a punk rocker with dyed hair, a tattoo and a laundry list of girls waiting for him back home. I'm a mama's boy. But we both had OCD, which made us brothers.

My unorthodox PlayStation ERPs returned in Boston, which raised a lot of curious eyebrows, and I answered a lot of questions about this unusual method of treatment.

"Why is Asher playing games during ERP when I'm licking this doorknob?!" (Real situation, by the way.)

I felt guilty about these things, and truthfully, it hurt my ERPs' effectiveness. But I can't deny how odd my treatment was.

My type of OCD is classified as "intrusive thoughts" in OCD context, which is the most ambiguous type. Typically, "contamination" OCD has to do with germs. "Checking" OCD has to do with making sure something is done or not done. "Hoarding" OCD refers to keeping things that have no use. "Symmetry" OCD is about all things being balanced. (Looking at you, Thanos.)

These are broad summaries, but for the most part, they apply. Intrusive thoughts OCD is 100 percent mental and can measure all over the spectrum of anxiety, obsessions, compulsions and all the causes and effects of mental illness.

In Boston, I started to make a concerted effort to integrate my ERPs into everyday activities. Even during downtime, when we didn't have to do ERPs, I did them.

My new motto became, "Every moment is an opportunity to get better."

I started taking my obsessions everywhere with me. That could be my odd photo collection or my demented audio tapes. When I watched TV, played video games, read a book, went on a walk – anything – I brought my curse with me. I started facing the discomfort on a full-time basis. I had to learn how to live with it.

I would post the pictures on walls, or on the sides of the TV screen. I remembered how I thought Reggie was embarrassing me by putting up my pictures at Menninger. I eventually saw how effective that was, and now I was willing to risk the awkward questions from others to have those pictures right in my face as often as I could.

I still tiptoed around the hardest, most anxious fears, but the constant, deliberate exposure was helping a lot in my treatment. My ERP was always a part of me anyway, so I literally made it *always* a part of me.

***

When I arrived at McLean, I had my own room for a week, but then I was moved. Not a big deal, as pretty much everyone at the hospital had a roommate. The problem, I soon realized, was that my roommate Sam turned out to be a legendary snorer.

I admit that I'm a notoriously poor sleeper, but this was unbearably bad. I could not sleep at all. It was so loud and so constant, and I would literally scream at him in the middle of the night so he would wake up. In that five-minute window before he started again, I tried to fall asleep.

It didn't happen, and the cycle continued nightly. I felt bad about yelling at him and interfering with his own sleep, but now it was affecting us both. I asked if I could sleep on the rec room couch, which was an easy no. I requested to switch rooms and brought it up constantly with my on-site therapist, but nothing ever changed.

Some nights, I even tried to fall asleep on the toilet, but you had to get staff permission to use the bathroom, so that was implausible on many levels.

The staff recommended ear plugs, then headphones, then meditation, and then all three. One of my most noteworthy memories of McLean is the sheer lack of sleep.

Sorry, Sam. You were a good dude. It wasn't your fault.

The days at McLean were a mixed bag. Every patient's treatment was a deciding factor in team morale. We couldn't, and eventually stopped trying to rely on staff for emotional support, so we looked to each other, which was fine. Almost all of us were very close. But if someone had a bad day, and a bad day in treatment does not go unnoticed, it affected the entire team.

On those days, people spent most of their time in their rooms. It's like in school when a kid gets in trouble, and the rest of the class only watches as they face their punishment. It's awkward, it's draining, and it's not a healthy environment to be in.

I started taking a lot of walks, which was something I needed to do anyway. We didn't exercise much at McLean, and I was still eating a lot on my medicine. I continued to gain weight, and that was (literally) feeding my unhappiness.

I took long walks with my iPod playing a mix of Maroon 5, Green Day, The Killers and some of my other favorites. For all the bad in this time of my life, catching up on years of music I had missed was a good thing.

The power of music cannot be understated. Just like my previous times in treatment, music was great therapy. Walking and music are a winning combo I still utilize today. Plus, Boston in the summer is absolutely beautiful.

A lot of my afternoons were spent watching Red Sox games or playing my video games like I did in ERP. While in ERP, gaming was intentionally stressful, a vehicle for me to try and mix hobbies and obsessions. When I wasn't in ERP, it had become something I still didn't always look forward to. Especially now that I was treating ERP as an all-day, everyday affair.

I just kept telling myself, "Every moment is an opportunity to get better."

***

For the sports fans out there, you may remember that 2011 was something of an eventful year for the Dallas-Ft. Worth metroplex.

For the first time since 2006, the Dallas Mavericks were back in the NBA Finals. Coincidentally, I was also back in treatment. I was able to attend some of the playoff games during the first couple rounds of the Mavs' 2011 run, but I was back in treatment by the end of May, when Dirk and the gang were on the verge of eliminating the Oklahoma City Thunder in the Western Conference Finals.

There was zero chance of me returning home to attend any of the NBA Finals games, but I was determined to make the best of watching them from afar. In a strange way, when I was miles and miles from home, I felt more connected to my local teams than ever.

I was fortunate to be able to watch all the Mavericks' Finals games. Sometimes I had the rec room, but the local Boston Bruins were in the NHL Stanley Cup Finals, so I was mostly relegated to the tiny television set in the main corridor.

Like the Bruins, the Mavs would go on to win the championship. The night the Mavs won should have been one of the best nights of my life – and in hindsight, it was – but it was one of my worst nights in treatment.

When the Mavs won, I was, well, I really can't put it into words. My dedication to the Mavericks was lifelong, and I poured my heart and soul into cheering for that team. After the final buzzer, Mavs star and mythical being Dirk Nowitzki sprinted off the floor and into the locker room, overwhelmed by emotion.

Comparing my situation with Dirk's is silly, but I felt the same way. In a life that took so much from me, seeing Dirk, Jason Terry, Tyson Chandler and the Mavs win an NBA championship gave me hope. Like, genuine hope. Not a "today the sun is out and it's going to be a good day" kind of hope – hope like, "Maybe I can beat this thing like the Mavericks beat the Heat."

On the surface, it's corny, but tell that to a teenager who's living with a mental illness in a hospital 2,000 miles from home and just saw his favorite team make the improbable climb to the top of the NBA mountain. Anything seemed possible after that.

In the moments that followed the Mavericks' triumph, I was humbled by reality. The McLean staff instructed me to go to bed, simultaneously giving half-hearted congratulations as if they had no idea the magnitude of what had just happened. But I begged for a few more minutes to watch the trophy ceremony.

Sure, they had no real obligation to let me watch it, and so they didn't. I pleaded my case, trying to explain this perhaps literal once-in-a-lifetime situation. Their response was to turn off the TV.

To paraphrase *Ferris Bueller's Day Off,* "Here's where Asher goes berserk."

I'm not proud of the hall-of-fame tantrum I put on at that moment. Do I regret it? I mean, when I think about putting my treatment at stake by yelling and screaming at a staff member that didn't want to deal with me anyway…

No. Not even a little bit. I deserved to watch that trophy ceremony, and I'll go to the grave thinking that.

Oh, man, did I lay into each and every member of the night staff that dared to cross my path. I felt like an ejected baseball manager who was just giving it to each umpire on his way off the field. I don't even remember how I ended up back in my room. In the moment, I thought they had taken this cherished memory away from me. But now I look back, and perhaps irresponsibly, give a nod of approval to 18-year-old me.

Another thing that sticks out from that night is a text I got from one of my friends. It was post-meltdown, and I was indeed in bed, on my phone without permission and exchanging celebratory messages with people back home.

My friend Ryan from one of my fantasy baseball leagues asked how I was going to celebrate.

"Party downtown?"

"Drink with your friends?" (I didn't drink then, don't worry, Mom.)

"Stay up all night!?"

I don't remember what lie I came up with, but I do remember sitting in bed, crying under the covers, listening to Sam play the nose flute and realizing how weird my life was.

Still, the Mavericks had won the NBA Finals.

The next day, I was in my therapist's office. To say he and I didn't see eye to eye would be an understatement.

True story: In my early days at McLean, he wanted to diagnose me as a closeted homosexual. One of my obsessions was an immature case of homophobia, which led him to that deduction. I guess that was his idea of treatment.

I am not homophobic now and I am an advocate for all human rights, LGBTQ+ included. But as a kid, I gave in to the societal fear of homosexuals, and a lot of my obsessive thoughts had to do with gay relationships.

I share this rare moment of specificity because this really did happen. The therapist at McLean – the one assigned to help me – wanted to diagnose me as a closeted homosexual. Because that's the first medicinal leap to take for a teenager who fears homosexuality.

About three weeks into my treatment, the night after my NBA Finals outburst, all my non-ERP TV and video game time had been suspended. I even had my social time restricted and was cut off from talking to some of the other patients.

An already tense relationship with the staff turned into an outrightly hostile one. I started to lose respect for their authority, and the prison-like environment in which they kept me now felt like an actual prison. I would sneak off to try and have conversations with Peter, Clark, Natasha or Bruce, and I'd have my punishment extended.

I told my parents about it, and they called the hospital to try and smooth things over, but my very immature self wasn't helping things from the inside. I refused to accept this punishment and further fractured a relationship that was on thin ice.

On the positive side, I was getting better, but I wasn't ready to go home. Bruce's prophetic words, shared with me in the bathroom on one of my first days in Boston, came rushing back to my attention. He said McLean had a very long waiting list, and as soon as they thought you were ready, they saw the potential for an open spot, rather than the need for any further treatment.

I thought it was the talk of paranoia at the time, but now I felt like they were looking for any reason to kick me out. And again, I wasn't helping by constantly questioning their judgment.

About a week after the infamous meltdown, I was playing *NBA 2K* during ERP. They couldn't take away my video game time during ERP because it was literally baked into my treatment plan.

I was called away by a doctor for just a moment, and when I came back, another patient had played my game and done irreparable damage to my team's fourth quarter lead.

Okay, this one, I will grant you, is silly.

Sure, my *NBA 2K10* Golden State Warriors franchise was in the playoffs. (That's right, I was on the Warriors train before they were the *Warriors*.) Anyone that knows me knows that I take my sports franchise gaming very, *very* seriously. I had gotten up to answer a question outside the rec room, and when I returned, this patient, who will go unnamed, had un-paused my game and turned a Warrior lead into a double-digit deficit.

Honestly, I was gone for like a minute. I don't know how he managed that kind of point swing in such little time – unless he did it on purpose. And in my mind, as immature or irrational or angry as you want to presume it was, it was intentional. Especially when this patient laughed in my face.

At this moment, about a week after the first incident, my anger, frustration and helplessness came to a boiling point. My first meltdown felt like a mere tease. I fully unleashed my inner Hulk.

And the next day, I was kicked out of the hospital.

Over that last week, things had not been going well for me at McLean. And I mean that personally and professionally. I was there to receive medical care, and I was making strides in that regard. However, I had cost myself a spot at the hospital through my behavior, the fallout continuing from that night on June 12th when the Mavericks won a championship.

My first feeling when they told me I was out was panic. I couldn't believe I was being thrown out of a medical facility. My second thought was, "My dad might *actually* kill me."

My parents were obviously very disappointed in me, as they should have been. But they were just as shocked that a hospital would discharge an ill, heavily medicated, emotionally unstable 18-year-old because of behavioral issues. It all felt petty to me, as if I had stood up to the man, challenged their authority and made myself an enemy in their eyes.

I make no excuses for my time at McLean being cut short. I don't regret my actions that came after the Mavericks' victory, but I do wish I'd handled the following week and then the *NBA 2K* incident like an adult – or at least a young one.

I was a very immature, inexperienced and newly minted 18-year-old. But I was still 18, and I didn't handle that situation well at all.

So, I came home, and man, it was tense.

For the first time in five hospital tours, the second in an inpatient setting and the first time at one since 2007, I left in a state of uncertainty. I was discharged on very regrettable terms, and though I tried to instill every bit of confidence in my parents that I was ready to come home, the reality was that I was not.

And so, even with the progress I made, it was yet another halfway measure. I came home, and I relapsed yet again.

To add insult to injury, when I returned home, my RoughRiders boss had had enough of my missed time. In his defense, in three summers I had missed at least a month of the season. Plus, my relationship with some of the other batboys did not improve.

I continued to refuse to do other people's work for them, and things got pretty crazy. The "main" batboy – so named because he worked there the longest and because his dad also worked in the organization – continued to deflect his own responsibilities onto other people's plates, mine included.

With what had just happened at McLean, coupled with the general chaos I face on a second-to-second basis, my patience for this kind of thing had gone from little to none.

One night, as Alex and I were getting ready to go to the pool for our customary trivia and swim, I was stopped by this guy and told to fill up his coolers for tomorrow's batting practice. Having already done mine, I refused. He proceeded to knock a full plate of mac and cheese out of my hand, spilling it all over the floor.

I quickly moved to clean it up, not wanting to draw any attention to myself, but next he knocked me to the ground and, at that point, even the players noticed. That's a big no-no. When you work in sports, you need to be invisible to the people who really matter.

We both got talked to by the clubhouse manager, but his behavior didn't stop. Soon after, when I again declined to fill up his coolers, he followed me out to my car and wouldn't let me get in and leave.

I then decided to bring it up to our boss. Two months later, when the season ended, three other batboys and I were fired. My former boss lost his job a year later, and the truly problematic batboy ended up getting fired himself soon after.

I was devastated at losing this job, as I loved baseball, but more importantly because I saw this job as a gateway to a future working in baseball. It hurt even more because the RoughRiders radio announcers had taken me under their wings and let me start spending game days in the booth with them when I wasn't working the field.

For the first time, I got to see baseball announcers work up close and personal. They even read my statistical notes and fun facts on the air. The respect that those two guys – Aaron Goldsmith and Brian Boesch – showed me has never been forgotten. That was one of the first moments I started to consider a career in sports broadcasting instead of sports journalism.

During my final months with the RoughRiders, I also started talking to the players more, something I was previously terrified to do. Most pro athletes have enough going on to talk to fans, let alone employees, but I was good about recognizing the correct moments.

I had so many cool, productive, baseball-minded chats with future MLB players like leadoff hitter Jemile Weeks, who told me the first pitch of the game is always the best pitch to hit.

Robbie Erlin and Joe Wieland were traded from the Texas Rangers to the San Diego Padres while both Double-A teams were playing in Frisco. I actually walked with them across the field from clubhouse to clubhouse.

Wil Myers and I talked about how he reminded me of one of my favorite players, Hunter Pence. I talked to Houston Astros minor leaguers J.D. Martinez and José Altuve about how I had lived in Houston. In late July, I told Martinez I thought he was getting called up to the majors soon. On July 30, he was.

My favorite games to work were the ones in which the RoughRiders played the San Antonio Missions, the affiliate of the Padres. Every time they were in town, I worked in the visitor's dugout. Players like Erlin, Wieland, brothers Cody and Jaff Decker, and especially pitchers Pedro Hernandez and Simon Castro, whom I'd spent most batting practice sessions with, treated me like one of their own.

Alas, it all came to an end in September 2011, but like many things in my life, I would return – that's a story for another time. Although, unlike the tale of how Maz Kanata came into possession of Luke Skywalker's lightsaber, you will eventually hear that story.

***

Crushed over the developments that had transpired in treatment and then with my job, I retreated into a dark hole in my life. Despite a year's worth of time, my world looked almost exactly the same as it did before I went to McLean in May.

That October, in a weird, continued trend of good things happening to Dallas sports teams, the Texas Rangers advanced to the World Series for the second straight year.

Up three games to two and one strike away from their first-ever championship, right on the heels of the Mavericks doing the exact same thing, my hometown baseball team pulled one of the biggest choke jobs in sports history.

The Rangers ended up losing the series in seven games to the St. Louis Cardinals, twice coming just one single pitch away from a title, and twice blowing it in epic fashion. People always ask me how I handled this as a sports fan. I tell people that I cried, which checks out on the believability scale.

But the truth was, I didn't even see it.

I was doing so poorly and, therefore, I was so medicated that I slept right through both games six and seven. And probably the rest. I did attend an ALDS game with my dad and an ALCS game with some friends, and I was able to hold it together enough to create some baseball playoff memories that year. However, I don't really tell people about my OCD, so the fact that I didn't even see the historic World Series game is something that I just shared for the first time.

2011 was a wild year.

CHAPTER 14

SUMMER 2012 – HOUSTON OCD PROGRAM

No, this isn't a typo, nor is it a repeat of Chapter 10. It's not a lazy Hollywood reboot, either.

Same place, different year.

My senior year of high school was a mess. I relapsed shortly after returning from Boston, and my time at school was as bad as it had ever been. What I remember most about my senior year is the amount of time I spent stuck at my locker.

Everything about my OCD peaked and, honestly, I stopped even trying to control it. I was so upset at the way things had transpired the year prior that I began to do something I told myself I would never do: give up.

I slacked off with my treatment, I missed a ton of school, and I spent most of my time at home just sitting on the couch in an endless cycle of mental rituals. Sometimes, I didn't even get to the couch and would be in hour-long trances while standing up. I was completely exhausted, and I felt like a zombie just going through the motions.

I talked less, I wrote less, I didn't even try going to class instead of BASE, and my already struggling relationship with my parents took an even bigger turn for the worse. My dad and I only saw each other when he had to drag me out of my paralysis and try to get me to school. I was so ashamed of where I was that I couldn't even face my mom.

My home life was rough. Both my siblings were away at college, and I didn't ever want to talk to either of my parents. It wasn't a good time.

At this very low point, I even started cutting my wrists. I did it privately and only subtly to avoid any real damage. I used scissors and didn't go very deep, so nobody would notice. I knew how wrong this was and told no one.

As part of my hopelessness, and due to always being stuck in place at home, I gained more and more weight. My trips to the local rec center had been sacred, but now I wouldn't chance it. I couldn't handle the anxiety. Nothing I did gave me any pleasure, so I just did nothing.

That was my senior year. Not exactly *High School Musical* material.

Even though I had lost just about all hope, my parents had not. They still wanted me to have a life, and I'll always be in their debt for not giving up on me. Keeping me in treatment facilities annually was very expensive. But to them, it was what had to be done.

Since I was of age, we felt that the Houston OCD impatient program had become the best option. Going to McLean had less to do with Houston not working, and more with wanting to try something new. I had never been to the Houston OCD Program as an inpatient, and the trip I was about to take would change my life.

***

There wasn't a whole lot to celebrate about completing high school. I didn't even go to my graduation.

The momentous day the final bell rang on my senior year, I wasn't even in school. I had finished my exams early, and on the day my peers celebrated the end of high school, my parents and I were in the car en route to Houston.

It was treatment round six, and we were going for the knockout.

I remember how sad I was, how lonely and depressed I felt. I was unhealthy on the inside and the outside. My parents refused to surrender to this life, even if I was wanting to shut down. My doctors thought that having school behind me would give me a renewed focus and perspective on not just my treatment, but also my life.

That may have played a role, but what really drove me was my parents – not just their belief in me, which I've mentioned over and over, but I was really starting to see what this was doing to them. My treatment was about getting myself better, but the epiphany that I could not only do this thing for me, but for *them*, provided me with the loudest wake-up call.

A lot of factors went into it, but the fact that I was now at the best treatment place for OCD in the world, as an inpatient with no strings attached and no external distractions, proved to be a turning point in my story of mental illness.

Being an inpatient at the Houston OCD Program was a night-and-day difference from my two ventures there as an outpatient. Being under their constant watch, guidance and mentorship, and having their complete trust to share anything and everything at any hour of the day – all of this empowered me and my treatment.

It's something I had felt before, but in Boston I had these self-realizations in isolation. Now, I was able to experience these moments of clarity, and I was able to *share* them.

The most important part of any therapy, perhaps even the most important part of being *human*, is talking about your feelings. I can physically see the eyes rolling when those words are said. But it's as true as anything I've ever experienced in life.

You have to talk about your feelings. But for this to happen, you must have people to talk to. For the six years leading up to the Houston OCD Program, I had Dr. Abel. But I even kept things from him, knowing he would force me to confront them.

Surrounded by the perpetually devoted staff and other determined patients, however, I found myself more open than ever. Sure, I did my ERPs as hard as I could, but I had done that before. To realize that the big thing I was missing in myself, and in my life, was getting in touch with my feelings…

Oh man, did I have some apologies to make to Dr. Abel.

He had implored me to do this for years, but I always beat around the bush. It's not easy to talk about your feelings, to expose yourself to that vulnerability and feel like you are small because you crave companionship and a listening ear. This self-discovery of talking – and doing it so casually with people who were also fighting this insane OCD battle – was like I had been slapped in the face by the truth.

I started to refer to "treatment" as "therapy." When my mom called, which she did every single day at the exact same time, she asked how treatment was going. She was elated to hear that I was now calling it therapy, and that therapy was going very well.

Of course, she and my dad and my whole family had reason to question my honesty. But I believe they could hear it in my voice. My dad would say, "You're starting to sound like you again," and nobody knew better than him.

I woke up every day eager to undergo my therapy and show those around me, and myself, that I was making actual, real-life progress. It wasn't pretend this time, and all my vulnerabilities were out in the open. I felt alive and held nothing back.

Each morning, I would burst out of bed; say "good morning!" to another patient, James, who lived across the hall; and then walk down the stairs to Darth Vader's "Imperial March" blaring through my phone. I felt like a big man on campus, a first for me and in a rather unusual setting.

I also befriended another housemate, Chad, who had traveled across the pond from England for treatment. Meeting someone my age who was fighting the good fight was always a plus, but we also had a lot of fun spending the summer trying to convince each other which sport was better: baseball or soccer.

Our conclusion? They are both boring, and we love them.

Sometimes, I started to get a little too excited and would crash a bit and get down. But at least I was having highs, and learning how to manage them was something I was more than happy to do. In therapy, it was important to stay level-headed.

Even on a good day, I needed to remember I was still in a place surrounded by people spending every moment on improvement. Just because *I* was having a good day didn't mean others were. That was a role reversal for me, and I learned to extend the same help and courtesy others had extended me when I was down.

Sometimes they took it, sometimes they didn't. I would be a hypocrite to not see that as normal behavior.

But as I improved, I started to take a leadership role amongst the patients. I was just 19, but I had a lot of experience in this particular field. It meant a lot to me that others, no matter their age, respected my history and allowed me to be of help, and the staff recognized it in me once I started to better conquer my obsessions.

***

The environment at the Houston OCD Program truly felt like a family. We went out to dinner together, and we had movie nights at the house, where I proudly hosted a *Star Wars* marathon. One of my prized possessions then – and still now – is my *Star Wars: The Complete Saga* Blu-ray set that was released in 2011. I brought it with me to Houston for many reasons, some of them ERP-related. At this point in my life, I was watching *Episodes I–VI* at least once a month. Even my love of *Star Wars* had its use for ERP.

"Every moment is an opportunity to get better."

OCD doesn't pause. It is always, and so became ERP.

Crossing hobbies with ERP was my most prominent method of therapy, and over the summer of 2012, the staff wanted me to face more exposures *outside* of the house. They knew I loved baseball, and being in Houston, I had started to follow the hometown Houston Astros. With my parents' permission, my new ERP became attending Astros games at Minute Maid Park.

The objective was simple: Every time you catch yourself falling into a mental ritual – or getting stuck – make a note. Did you fall into the anxiety "trap," or did you let it go? The goal was to tally how many times I let my obsessions become compulsions, versus how many times I could deal with the anxiety and enjoy the game.

I continued to walk almost every day as well, and there was a basketball court nearby. I can't tape pictures of my obsessions to the Astros dugout or bring them to the park, but I did have my audio tape. My gold Sony Walkman CD player made its way all over the Space City.

Even without pictures or audio for ERP, "bringing my thoughts with me" was never an issue. We can't turn our brains off.

A bad habit I had with my thoughts while playing sports was feeling the need to repeat an action when I had a bad thought, just as I did with tics and repetition. On a basketball court, this meant making the same shot over and over and over again. Depending on how long I let the ritual chain become, sometimes this meant making as many as a dozen or more shots in a row. That number would grow if I didn't reach it in one try. This cycle destroyed shooting hoops at home for me, and now that I had honestly brought that up with the Houston staff, they sent me to the park to work on this form of ERP.

This also helped me get exercise, and going to Astros games allowed me to do something I never did anymore back in Plano: Get out of the house!

At this time, the Astros were absolutely terrible, which somehow made me fall in love with them. I resonated with the fact that the Astros were completely starting over. Management had torn the organization completely apart; traded my favorite player, Hunter Pence; and entered a historically deep rebuild.

They were the worst team in baseball. The Astros were the only team in 2012 not to win 60 games, winning only 55. Nobody went to the games, and this made tickets very, very cheap. I bought $5 nosebleed seats and moved down to the very first row behind the dugout.

Ushers didn't care. They were probably wondering why I wanted to get *closer* to the action.

There were so few people at the game, and it was so quiet, that the players would turn around and talk to me. I remember having conversations in the middle of the game with players like Bud Norris, Brett Myers, Jason Bourgeois, J.A. Happ, Jordan Schafer (whose walk-up song was "Call Me Maybe," which is awesome) and many charismatic others.

It was a blast. Having fun only made the therapy part of it more powerful. When I'm enjoying myself, OCD is much more of a threat. If I'm bored to tears and somewhere I don't want to be, my thoughts are exponentially less intrusive.

Growing up a Rangers fan, it was very weird becoming an Astros fan, too. At the time, the Astros were in the National League, and rooting for them was of little consequence to my fandom. Plus, at this time, I started to become less interested in specific teams and more passionate about the overall game of baseball.

As far as other sports went, I started watching my hometown teams less, except for a focus on the Mavericks, which still survived despite owner Mark Cuban's best efforts to destroy Dirk Nowitzki's happiness by surrounding him with mediocre players following the championship.

In baseball, however, I started to focus on four teams: the Rangers, the Astros, the Miami Marlins (my mom's hometown team and my grandpa's favorite), and the San Francisco Giants, the team that played in my favorite park and in the city where my aunt lived.

My entire life had improved that summer. My OCD got better, obviously, but my happiness was at a place it had not been since before my very first symptom way back in 2006. I wish I could say this is the end of the story, and while it is the end of an era in my life, my journey was far from over.

I like to think of my life as a superhero movie: Even when the hero wins, he must give up a part of himself to do it, like Batman in *The Dark Knight* when he sacrifices his career and legacy for the common good of Gotham. Or Spider-Man trading love for heroism.

I could go on. Don't worry, I won't.

As I departed Houston for the fourth and – spoiler alert – final time, I'll always remember what Gelani, one of my most trusted counselors, doctors, confidants and friends, told me on the way out.

"Asher, we love you. But I never want to see you again."

That was the last thing anyone ever said to me at the Houston OCD Program, a place I had been to three times in four years, and four times in six years counting Menninger.

He said those memorable words, smiled, gave me a big hug, and I was gone.

CHAPTER 15
FALL 2012 – COLLEGE

When my doctors said that being relieved from the pressure of high school would help my therapy, they were right. That summer back home in 2012 was the smoothest few months I'd had in a long, long time.

How could it not be with *The Avengers*, *The Dark Knight Rises* and *The Amazing Spider-Man* all coming out?!

I even got a small job as a freelance sports journalist at a Dallas company called YouPlus. (A woman in the office traveled to London to cover the 2012 Summer Olympics, so yeah, credibility.)

Every day, I drove from my house to the DART station across town, then rode the train to Dallas, walked another 20 minutes to a small office building and wrote about sports for five hours or so.

It was a cool experience, except for riding the DART and having a stranger behind me run his fingers through my hair, but such are the adventures of Dallas public transportation. The job paid little but was more about the experience and getting my name and content out in a credible way.

I was also invited by my old friend at Menninger, Dr. Thröstur Björgvinsson, or just Dr. B, to speak at an OCD event in Dallas. Beyond honored, I humbly accepted.

I had come a long way, but still had so much longer to go. Still, it was a rewarding experience to tell people there's a light at the end of the tunnel, even if I was still in the tunnel myself.

Then summer ended, and I couldn't hide from school forever. Or at least I didn't *want* to.

Going to a four-year university was out of the question because of my high school results, but nearby Collin College was one of the more respected community colleges around. I would still live at home, so going to college would basically be like going to high school. For this reason, I was nervous.

College is a big step in anyone's life. For me, this was trial by fire after not getting a proper high school experience. Stepping back into real life, outside of the structure of treatment, was a haunting proposition. But like death, taxes or the Dallas Cowboys losing a playoff game, it was unavoidable.

My first few weeks at Collin went okay. I was attending class and doing the bare minimum to get by. Collin had a sort of quasi-special ed program that I was registered in, but it was harder to use as a commuter than if I had been on campus all day.

Plus, the BASE system in high school – and most support systems in K-12 – are built to help you. College programs are built to *support* you. After all, you're kind of on your own in college.

Still, I made a promise to myself that I would honor Gelani's word. I would never see him again, except maybe at an Astros game. I would never be in treatment for OCD again. I was determined, no matter what, not to let that happen.

So, I brought home my unfiltered honesty and gave it to Dr. Abel. I still kept the sordid details out of conversations with my parents, but I wasn't going to lose my improved communication skills I had worked so hard on in therapy.

My sessions with Dr. Abel were still twice a week, and they continued to be very productive. We did ERPs together to ensure I would not slack, and I gave him reports about my progress at home.

I was tired of letting people down, and that included him. Since 2007, he had been there for me, as much as I would let him. Same with my parents, but with Dr. Abel, I was as open and honest as I had ever been.

This helped, and with my OCD, I continued to stay afloat. I still got stuck, but it was less often. I still got stressed, but it was less frequent.

I committed to two things: ERP and school. They were both going okay, particularly the former, and when my OCD started to finally subside after all these years, I was faced with a life that I had done very little with since 6th grade.

I tried to branch out, get back into social settings, but I was still on a lot of medication at that point. I managed to keep a friend, Jake, but he was off living his best life at the University of Texas.

Most days strictly consisted of school and therapy. I was so worn out from these fundamental tasks, and in combination with heavy medicine, the only other thing I did a lot of was sleep.

I had video games and movies, and I can't tell you how much *Family Guy, American Dad!* and *Archer* I watched from 2012–2014.

But I was craving a social life.

I had been stuck in ice like Captain America for seven years, and when I came out, I didn't recognize the world, and it didn't recognize me.

It all seems a tad melodramatic, but the intensity of loneliness I felt was so high. I started to let this affect me. Just as OCD picked on me at my low moments, the other parts of mental illness like anxiety and depression began to attack me – and in the strongest ways that they ever had.

***

Come September, I was in a vulnerable state. Then, my grandfather passed away. My father's father Harry had been battling Alzheimer's for years, but his death was still sudden. Harry, or "Papa," was the ultimate socialite and beloved by all.

The best proof of this was his funeral. Rather than a somber gathering of family, it was a celebration of his life attended by all who adored him. We laughed, we cried, we shared stories, and there were more tears of joy than there were of sadness.

I had been so sick for so long that I was out of touch with my family. The relationship with my immediate family was strained, and I didn't see as much of my extended family as I should have. I wish I did. I wish I could see Papa and his wife Geema one more time. They were two of my biggest fans, and I wish they could see me today.

Every birthday, Geema typed and printed every grandchild a personalized birthday card. The last one she wrote me was in 2014, and she predicted that 2015 would be my "best year ever."

She was right.

At the same time as Papa's passing, my other grandmother, my mother's mother in Miami, was not doing well. She was suffering from Lewy body dementia. A woman known for being the ultimate caretaker had been reduced to a vegetative state and required 24/7 care.

It was very difficult to deal with, especially for my mom. My mom flew down to Florida every few weeks, adding another must-do task to her already overflowing schedule.

Before my grandmother passed away in 2016, I made a couple of trips with my mom, especially when I was doing better. I helped take care of Grandma and went to Marlins games with my grandpa, my uncle and some cousins.

I was blessed with four incredible grandparents. They passed away in 2012, 2015, 2016 and 2017. After 2015, I was well enough to make them a part of my life again. I made a commitment to keep in closer touch, especially since I was unable to see them as much as I would have wanted when I was struggling.

I started to call my grandpa every Friday. The stereotype that kids don't want to call their grandparents didn't apply to him – it was quite the opposite. I didn't have to hang up on him, he'd hang up on me. As kind as he was, he was a man of few words.

With my OCD situation, I hardly left the house. I didn't see enough of my grandparents, and I'll always wish I could go back and change that.

***

The thing about having a mental illness is that it's always *something*. When an obsession starts to loosen its grip on you, something else pops up. When my OCD had at last become manageable, my anxiety was heightened, and my depression became intense.

I started taking medicine not just for OCD, but for anxiety and a level of depression that was scaring me and my family, as it started to send me back toward an immobility I hadn't shown since returning from Houston.

Keeping up with school became a more difficult task, and I felt pressure to hold off the impending doom that I had experienced so many times before. I was tired of this cycle repeating itself and, frankly, I was pissed off with it.

I was doing my ERPs. I was doing the work. But now I was just so damn sad all the time.

I talked to my doctor about it. I even opened up to my parents about it because the depression was so strong. We looked at different medications to try that might keep me level and in school. Our most important objective outside of my health was keeping me in school.

For however much it helped, the side effects were getting bad again. I ate more and more and continued to put on weight. I was embarrassed of my appearance and didn't want to go out.

My relationships at home began to strain again, especially with my parents' attention focused solely on me, since none of my siblings were around. At least they got to take a family trip to London the summer I was in treatment. They definitely deserved it.

Turning in classwork went from a hopeful occurrence to a rare feat, and after a semester of school, I dropped out. I didn't even realize this until years later, but I only managed one course credit (three hours) in my first semester of college.

I was so ashamed of my life – and so determined to avoid my parents – that I spent afternoons at a nearby Starbucks, pretending to write and chugging down Frappuccinos with their money. At home, I stopped eating dinner with them and became hateful toward my dad's signature grilled chicken and salmon. I wanted junk, and I ate a lot of it. When they refused to pay for it, I screamed and shouted and threw things until they either gave in, or I just went to sleep.

On one particularly ridiculous occasion, I had a friend from my fantasy sports leagues order Jimmy John's online and send it to my home address. He lives in South Carolina.

As 2013 approached, I was pushing 185 pounds. Things were once again spiraling out of control, and I wasn't letting anyone help.

I thought I had pledged to never let this happen again. I had conquered the worst part of my OCD to honor that promise. I had experienced anxiety and depression before, but without most of my attention on OCD, the intensity and despair of these new feelings overwhelmed me in a new way.

Why was I letting this happen again? Hadn't I learned my lesson over and over?

I've asked myself this countless times over the years. Even today, I wonder what I could have done differently. I asked Dr. Abel and Dr. Robinson hundreds of times, and something Dr. Robinson said years ago to my parents, something I wasn't told until a few years ago, stands out.

"Asher has one of the most severe cases of mental illness I have ever seen," he said. "The truth is, he will never get over it. It will always be a part of him.

"But the hope, and the goal, is not that he does get over it. But he learns to live with it, and it doesn't control him."

And the part I remember most:

"The best treatment for Asher is *time*. As he gets older, he will get better. At times, he will get worse. But in the end, he *will* get better."

Dr. Robinson said this to my parents around 2008 or 2009. Honestly, I don't know the exact date. I wasn't told until a couple years ago. What he said is undeniably true, and I believe in my heart that this is why my parents put up with all of my relapses over the years.

They held out hope for my life that even if our days together were hell in the present moment, that eventually the sun would shine on our family again.

I'm glad they did continue to believe in me, because if they had given up, I wouldn't have had anywhere to go. And this is what countless many with mental illnesses face. None of us relapse on purpose.

None of us *choose* this.

One thing I asked my parents time and time again was the familiar question of "why" I had this… this thing. I begged them to find a brain surgery and just take out whatever caused this. There had to be a way, right? Well, there wasn't, still isn't, and there won't be for a long time, if ever. That's just the nature of this beast.

So, when I continued to fall on my face again and again, and my life went back into the very dark place it had been so many times before, people still held out hope, even if I didn't.

CHAPTER 16
2013 – A LOST YEAR

For so many years, I had dealt with my OCD in just about every way possible. But depression was new, and it was scary. While I had built a trusty toolkit of ways to combat the mental illness that I had lived with for seven years, I had no personal ways to deal with depression.

Dr. Abel was my biggest ally in the fight, along with my parents. I would completely open up to him, and he would do his best to help me. At first, I felt like I would be able to handle it, as I had handled so much already, but this was something entirely different.

Any time I felt like I was working well with my depression, the OCD would kick into higher gear. If I managed the OCD well, then my depression would put a quick, swift check on any happiness I felt. Together, OCD and depression were like Kevin Durant and Russell Westbrook: a duo that only created chaos.

Another one of my many "isms" I developed through the years – I often think I had early onset adulthood in my life – is that "mental illness never lets you be happy."

In the moments of mental clarity, when you just want to sit down and do something mindless like play video games, you can't. The mind never, ever, ever shuts off, and even if I was having a good day, any happiness or peace I felt would seem like a temporary cheat code from one of my games.

In simple, non-medical terms: It frickin' sucked. Every day sucked. At some point, I just started to believe once more that this was my lot in life, and I was just to do with it the best I could. School wasn't meant to be, I would never get along with my family, and my only escapes to the real world would be momentary.

It was not a good way to live, but it was living. And there were many times I questioned even that, much to the horror and sadness of those close to me.

In the summer of 2013, I was not doing well. The previous year, the family had taken a trip to London while I recovered stateside. This time, even in my volatile state, I would be joining the gang on another overseas trip.

***

A quick interjection for a travel story that has a *happy* ending. In April 2013, amid all the usual chaos, my wonderful Aunt Linda, who is the reason I am a San Francisco Giants fan, somehow convinced my folks to let me fly out to San Francisco – by myself – for the Giants' Opening Day.

With my Buster Posey jersey on, and a Hunter Pence shirt added at the gift shop, this was and still is my favorite trip I have ever taken.

The Giants were coming off a 2012 World Series win, so Opening Day, which is a holiday even when you're *not* celebrating a championship, was an incredible experience. The ferry ride to the park, the garlic fries at the then-named AT&T Park – as previously noted, my favorite venue in all of sports – the breathtaking scenery of the bay… what a few days that was.

Fast-forward to June and to what should have been the trip of a lifetime – well, it was for everyone else, but it turned into a trip from Hell for yours truly.

***

I've never liked to travel. The whole process stresses me out to no end. I hate going to the airport, being at the airport, waiting at the airport, waiting more at the airport, and I'm terrified of planes (though that has gotten better over time). Did I mention I hate the airport? It seems like everyone is the worst version of themselves at the airport.

It's crowded, it's rushed, it's smelly, it's stressful, it's unnerving, it's just… uncomfortable. My family is particularly difficult to travel with, though we've made great improvements, especially after my sister introduced her husband Adam to the unit.

My dad's internal clock runs at a million miles an hour, and my mom, well, hers doesn't. On top of that, we seem to run into the worst luck on our trips. If there is a weather delay, or plane repairs, or lost luggage, it's probably happening to the Feltmans.

I do not like to travel.

In 2013, I was still terrified of flying, which didn't help. I wasn't doing very well with my OCD, I was severely depressed, I wasn't getting along with anyone in my family, and now we were taking an international trip together for two weeks.

What could go wrong?

In plain terms, I did not want to go, which I know sounds terribly spoiled. "Oh, poor me! I don't want to go to Spain or Rome or see the Amalfi Coast!" It wasn't bad enough that I was dead weight, but I got as sick as I've ever been when we were in Amalfi. I was blowing chunks out of both ends, which was as good a time as any to discover a bidet.

When we got home, things only got worse. The trip was a disaster for me, and all I did was cause everyone else problems instead of being a part of these incredible memories.

Returning to my black hole, I was out of school and out of touch. My parents pushed me to do something – anything – and that something and/or anything ended up being a job.

Thus began the Asher Feltman employment carousel, which would travel the DFW metroplex far and wide over the next six years. If the great Johnny Cash *went* everywhere, I *worked* everywhere.

When I was in really bad shape, literally and figuratively, from 2012–2014, I wasn't helping myself in terms of my diet. I ate a lot of crap, and Sonic was on that list. Not to call Sonic as a whole "junk," because their 2–4pm "Happy Hour" is one of the greatest gifts ever bestowed on mankind. But you don't go to Sonic for a salad.

I figured that was a solid place to work, and I could get paid extra for doing the whole retro drive-in roller-skating bit. My first mistake was assuming I still knew how to skate. I was a champ at all the Thunderbird Roller Rink birthday parties back in the day, but that was years ago. Also, I think the extra-pay-for-skating thing is a myth.

Not that I would really know because I worked at Sonic for two days.

My 2013 really was a waste – that's why I call it "a lost year." The lights even went out at the Super Bowl. And *Man of Steel* should have been good.

I did nothing, I accomplished nothing, I went backward, and worst of all, I made life difficult for those who cared about me.

The relationships around me continued to sour, especially with Mom and Dad, who pushed and pushed and pushed to get me to do anything with my life. I got frustrated with my doctors and my parents, my biggest supporters, when the real person holding me back was the man in the mirror.

Toward the end of the year, I ventured back out into the job market and got hired at Studio Movie Grill. I started in December, went on our annual family trip, and then came back to realize the manager didn't know I was leaving town, and I had missed several shifts.

I was pretty messed up at the time, but I swear I told him I was leaving town. That job was a nightmare anyway. I was 20, working at a movie theater with high school kids who didn't want to work. I busted my tail so hard at SMG that my sweat would drip into the soda cups I was carrying for customers, sending me back to the kitchen over and over. At least I got free meals at the end of the night, but that wasn't exactly helping me fight the weight battle I was losing.

By the end of 2013, I weighed almost 200 pounds.

CHAPTER 17

2014, PART 1 – A DARK NIGHT

Looking back, 2014 might have been the most important year of my life. Like years past, there were ups and downs, but these ups and downs were up like Chewbacca and down like R2-D2.

After a few uneventful months that looked and felt like my soulless 2013, I got another job. I went where the stuff is right, the prices are low, and back support is a no – the sporting goods store, Academy Sports & Outdoors. Working there was probably my least favorite job I'd ever had. But unlike Sonic and Studio Movie Grill, I actually held on to this position for a while!

Two months or so.

Working a cash register doesn't sound like the most fun thing to do, and I can confirm even without sources that, no, it isn't. And standing in one spot for hours at a time, especially when you are 50 pounds overweight, does not feel good. It was my fault for being fat, but still, couldn't a guy get a break at some point?

My first job of 2014 didn't tickle my fancy, but it was the first eventful thing to happen to me in this important year. However, the most important thing to happen to me that year – and maybe in my life – was Captain America.

Finding happiness is the key to living. Who said that? You? Me? Every motivational speaker ever? Doesn't matter. What matters is that, no matter how corny, cheesy, childish or innocent something may seem, *all that matters* is your happiness. Will Smith didn't pursue it for nothing.

My source of joy for most of my life had come from my heroes. Some real, some fantasy. But the impact that real heroes like Dirk Nowitzki and Frank Catalanotto, or fictional ones like Spider-Man and Batman had on me in my formative years is undeniable.

We all need heroes.

Like Aunt May said in *Spider-Man 2*, "I believe there's a hero in all of us, that keeps us honest, gives us strength, makes us noble." I believe this in my heart to be true. And for me, finding a reason to smile went a long, long way.

Unfortunately, the sports world was losing its magic. As I got older, I started to realize that professional sports are not about the fans, the players, the memories or even winning. It's all about money. Over time this has become even truer. Gone are the glory sports days of the 80s, 90s and 2000s, and it wasn't just me getting older or sicker that was making me come to this realization.

I genuinely believe the product in the NBA and MLB, my two favorite sports leagues as a kid, are a shell of their former selves. Now, I'm not here to debate that (though I will), but as my passion for sports started to dwindle, I searched even harder for something to give my life joy.

Thankfully, I found it.

***

It's no secret that I grew up a fan of superheroes. Sci-fi, fantasy, fiction, my love for *Star Wars*, it's all been there. I just never really did much with this passion.

I never really did, well, anything.

In my years of stasis, I would literally sit in bed until the early afternoon, go to the couch and stare at the wall until the evening, and then try and sleep my way until the next tomorrow.

Before this, if you remember from your earlier reading, times were better. Way back in 2004, my friend Pierce and I went to see *Spider-Man 2* in theaters seven times.

A year later at Jake's birthday party, *Revenge of the Sith* and the *Star Wars* saga were introduced into my life.

In 2005, the *Dark Knight* trilogy was born, and in 2008 came the Marvel Cinematic Universe (MCU). If I had any escape in my life whatsoever, it was these movies and these characters. They distracted me from my painful existence, but I never needed these films and worlds as much as I did in 2014.

I had gotten increasingly into the MCU movies, especially without any new *Star Wars* or Batman movies. I always had a passion for reading and would read a lot as a kid, especially the *A Series of Unfortunate Events* books. If there was a long car ride to go on, I brought one of Lemony Snicket's adventures.

As time went by and my brain had other priorities, reading was no longer a part of my life. But when I started re-discovering my passion for movies through the MCU, I also re-discovered my passion for reading.

I started picking up comic books left in right, finding their 22-page serial format perfect for my compromised attention span. I fell back in love with characters I'd always admired, like Spider-Man and Batman, but I really started to connect with Captain America.

Truthfully, I always found Captain America to be a bit of a square. I've written more about these things on my personal blog (stay tuned), but in the "Golden Age" of comics, aka in older comics, Cap was the guy who said things like, "Let's work together, team!" or, "Evil must not prevail!"

After the turn of the century, pretty much the entire Marvel comics roster got a rebrand, including the Star-Spangled Man. Courtesy of writer Ed Brubaker, Steve Rogers became the modern-day badass superhero that fans always dreamed of. The character's ascent to the top of my favorites list coincided directly with the next movie coming out from Marvel's growing universe: *Captain America: The Winter Soldier*.

On a bit of a whim, I bought opening-night tickets to a double feature that played *The Winter Soldier* and its predecessor, *Captain America: The First Avenger,* back to back. I never really went out – or did *anything* – so I think my parents were really happy I was actually leaving the house for a change.

That night at Cinemark in Plano was absolute heaven. It sounds ridiculous – and maybe it is, I really don't care, *people need heroes* – but I felt some sort of spiritual rebirth that night. I saw a hero on screen that was everything I wanted to be.

Obviously becoming a super soldier was out of the question, but I could still become a "super" version of Asher Feltman. I didn't even need to be super, but I needed to change. That night, I didn't just watch a movie, I was inspired to finally get off my ass and turn my life around.

This new inspiration led to a sit-down with my parents and Dr. Abel, and we explored possibilities for getting my life back on track. Full of newfound hope, I put going back to school on the table, but everyone felt that was a little too ambitious after crashing and burning in that department a short time ago.

At this point, my OCD was in a manageable state. I didn't need to go back to treatment. Rather, I needed some life support. The OCD was a formidable nuisance, but my depression and anxiety were causing the serious issues.

We ended up at a place in Dallas called Innovation 360. Innovation 360, or I360, is an addiction treatment center for young adults. I did not fall into that category, but the place was deemed compatible for my needs.

It felt reminiscent of my very first hospital visit eight years earlier, when I was admitted to the eating disorder wing at Children's Hospital in Dallas, because there was nowhere else to go.

Riding high on momentum, things started off promising at I360. I lived in a house with other patients and a rotation of counselors, many of them recovering addicts as well. I was a fish out of water in that sense, but nobody disagreed on the collective goal: self-improvement.

I was admitted sometime around April 10, 2014, about a week after the emotional awakening from *The Winter Soldier*. My memories at I360 start off with my roommate Clint, who did not have a drug addiction, but rather suffered from cerebral palsy. We hit it off and connected over our fondness of Houston, where he was from, and where I used to live. We both liked the Astros. He loved the Rockets. I didn't.

One of the first things I did while in the program was sit down and ask myself what I wanted to do in life. Before things went off the rails more than a year earlier, I was in school at Collin College pursuing a journalism degree.

Remembering that I wanted to be a sports journalist felt like someone had poked me with a stick and woken me from a long slumber. My love for sports wasn't what it used to be, but I still had a passion for it, and there was no reason not to pursue it.

I reconnected with some of my old writing contacts and began contributing to various websites. I started writing again about the Dallas Mavericks, Texas Rangers and Houston Astros for three different blogs. I was enjoying it.

My days were broken down by working at Academy and writing. There were few problems reacclimating to the career path I used to know. The problems – because when in my life have there not been any? – came from life in the I360 program.

***

The Innovation 360 program took place at a rented house in downtown Dallas off Mockingbird Lane. It was in an older neighborhood, and the house was, to put it lightly, disgusting. One of my chores was to clean the bathroom, and our community toilet was always covered in unspoken horrors that would strike fear into the hearts of young children.

The counselors were well-intentioned, but they were young and immature like we were. This wasn't a job they had to go to school for, and that's okay. But I felt that they didn't treat us the best, especially me, whose presence in the program was often questioned. To my face. You can't *see* mental illness, and truthfully, people asked me daily why I was even there. Trying to explain myself got old.

We spent a lot of time working out – definitely a way to improve yourself, but we would literally do tire flips at the local rec center like

30 minutes after eating a huge breakfast. In all my years of athletic competition, I don't remember puking after a single workout. But at 1360, the orange juice and French toast had no chance.

After about a week there, I got sick. I don't think it was the excessive workouts, but I'm not ruling out the things that were growing in our bathroom. Worst of all, the staff thought I was faking it to get out of the workouts or so I wouldn't have to go to my job at Academy, which they knew I didn't like.

Somewhere between working a sick shift and throwing up scrambled eggs, we had a volleyball outing that I asked if I could skip to stay in bed. They said I had to go, and I pushed back. So, instead of sitting it out and resting at home, they made me tag along. I was able to negotiate my way out of playing and watched feverishly from the sidelines.

I got into shouting matches with the other boys over things such as hygiene and responsibilities, but it was somehow always my fault. Simply put, I did not fit in at this place.

On April 26th, I was feeling better, and I bought a $200 ticket to the Mavericks playoff game against the San Antonio Spurs. My parents advised against that decision, as that amount equaled days of work for me, but I was feeling rebellious for a lot of reasons. Not to mention I had missed so many Mavericks playoff games due to treatment over the years.

This was game three of a first-round series against the Mavs' biggest rival, and it ended up being one of the greatest games in NBA Playoff history.

With seconds remaining, Vince Carter hit a miracle three-pointer from the corner to give Dallas a huge upset win at the buzzer. I mean, he traveled, but it's the NBA.

It was a glorious moment and the loudest I had ever heard the American Airlines Center, including the many years of peak Mavericks playoff contention. I hugged a bunch of people I didn't know, which is always a great sign at a sporting event.

After the game, going back to my temporary home and life, I was so excited to talk about what I had just witnessed — only nobody cared. Snide remarks about how I had suddenly felt better to go to the game were my greeting when I walked through the door. It was the usual passive-aggressive talk that I always got.

"Why is this guy even here?"

I was already on shaky ground with these guys, and several sarcastic remarks later resulted in a conference with the program's manager.

I voiced my concerns about what was happening, and I think I could physically see them going in and out of the guy's ears. It wasn't a happy relationship, and I was begging my parents to let me come home.

Naturally, they said no and that I needed to work through this. They didn't have the full picture of what was going on, and I can see how it looked like I was just being immature and complaining, especially after my theatrics in Boston three years earlier.

I was in a bad place. My depression and anxiety were roaring back, accompanied by an anger I did not recognize. My voice was not being heard. My cries for help were filed under complaints. My longing for change was translated to an unwillingness to participate.

It was bad.

On top of being sick and sad, I was overcome with rage. Progress was eluding me, and I was heading back into a dark place that I thought I had finally come out of a few weeks earlier.

About a week later, we were all watching the Mavericks and Spurs play game seven of the same series. The Spurs blew out the Mavs, and I was hearing it from everyone. I was in a fragile state already and really losing my cool.

Before the game even ended, we were shouting again, and they told me to go to my room. I did go to my room, but I grabbed my car keys, and without so much as making eye contact, raced angrily to my car parked out front.

I got inside, put the key in the ignition and decided I was going to kill myself.

CHAPTER 18

2014, PART 2 – TIMEOUT

When a big moment in your life happens, I feel like you either don't remember it until it's over, or you vividly remember it every step of the way. In this instance, for me, it was the latter.

Years ago, in one of my hour-long "stuck" episodes, I took a kitchen knife and threatened to use it on myself in front of my parents. But even at that moment, I was just frustrated. I wasn't going to do anything.

Even in those terrible moments that I cut myself, I never had any intention further than inflicting pain. I was used to feeling hopeless. I expected disappointment and, therefore, had trouble getting disappointed. I'd felt hopeless for as long as I could remember.

I'd been sick since 2006 and could count the good days in the last eight years on two hands. But the feeling I had on May 3, 2014, went beyond hopelessness. I wasn't just angry – I was angry *at life*. I was done trying to play whatever twisted game my existence was turning out to be.

For the very first time in all this time, I was planning on ending my life.

***

After racing through the house and getting in my car, I decided I would drive until I found something to hit. I screamed through a stop sign, making brief eye contact with a lady who later told police

I looked like I was about to do something bad. I drove fast, shouting in anger through a stream of tears, until, at last, I found something to hit.

I drove off road and went straight into a fence. Just a fence. Somebody's garden had become the only casualty of the day, and with their exterior fence wrapped around the front of my vehicle, I stopped my car, put it in park and continued weeping.

The next thing I remember was talking to the woman whose garden I had just destroyed. I remember an extremely relaxed, soft voice asking me if I was alright. Hyperventilating through tears, I couldn't even speak. I just wrote down a phone number and the word "mom."

Things were hazy after that, but the next person to arrive was a police officer. The scene was cleared, I was cuffed due to procedure, and they took me to a psychiatric ward for evaluation. This was a new low.

Oddly enough, I remember the police car ride. An impossibly short amount of time had passed since I left the 1360 house, and the Mavericks game was still going on. The officer had the game on the radio, and we talked about it momentarily. Even laughed a little. It was a surreal moment that felt like an out-of-body experience.

If there was a rock bottom for me, I had just hit it.

***

Over the next couple hours, I waited at the hospital and heard some of the most interesting, unbelievable tales from the other patients. I heard fascinating backstories, radical business proposals, and mind-blowing conspiracy theories. I learned from my new friends that I shouldn't trust the system. I got new clothes and some of those soft socks with the bumps on the bottom so that you don't slip and sat in an assigned chair.

I was terrified.

I had a psychiatric evaluation and was cleared, but they wanted me to stay the night. My parents had other ideas and took me home – home to Plano.

***

Of all the moments in my life, this one sticks out the most. I had been in a bad place for a long time, and I always questioned the "why" of my OCD, especially to Dr. Abel. We talked all the time about my situation, my emotions, my life and my future.

Through it all, and with the support of those who love me, I held out hope. I held out hope that, somehow, I could live with this thing. I didn't hold out hope that I would beat it, because a cure for OCD – as with so many other mental illnesses – remains a fantasy. I get that.

But it hadn't gotten to the point where I considered giving up. Or, as Dr. Abel phrased it, "giving in to the OCD."

On May 3rd, I did that. But deep down, I wanted to live. Or I would have made a much more legitimate attempt. I believe deep down that instead of driving into a brick wall, or into traffic, I went into a little fence and a garden for a reason.

Now, my parents ended up paying to repair that fence and garden, and of all the things that resulted from this horrible occasion, I really felt like crap about what I did to that kind lady's property. There was no criminal action taken, and we simply attempted to move on.

I had thought that my voice was no longer being heard. Honestly, my life *had* become a cycle of relapses, and everyone who was dedicating their lives to helping me was not having their faith rewarded.

But I also felt that no one was listening, that my cries for help were now akin to the infamous ones from "The Boy Who Cried Wolf."

I had put everyone through the same cycle of despair over and over. I guess I thought they had given up on me when that couldn't have been further from the truth.

It was time to put up or shut up – to show them, once and for all, *now or never*, that I was going to turn my life around.

CHAPTER 19

2014, PART 3 – A NEW HOPE

The next day, my dad drove me back to Innovation 360 to pick up
my belongings and move out. To put it lightly, this was awkward.
My dad, being the man of few emotional words he's always been,
didn't really say much about what I had done. I think it was better
that way.

I believe what I did was a cry for help. There was no intent, despite
the danger and the potential of something going very, very wrong.
I felt I was no longer being heard, and honestly, I had cried wolf so
many times that it was hard to tell what I really felt.

But what happened, happened. I got lucky, and it was time to
move on.

The first thing I did was find a new job. I wasn't formally fired
from Academy, but I also hadn't shown up to work in a while. For my
next job, I decided the last thing I wanted to do was stay in one spot
all day, so I got a job delivering pizzas at Domino's.

After getting lost on my first drive, I literally turned things around.
Domino's ended up not only being a good job, but a job that I stuck
with. Fourth time's the charm, I guess? Or fifth? I've already lost
count.

I made good money at Domino's, as thankfully this was 2014, so
Uber Eats did not exist. And I really did enjoy it. I dinged up my car
a few times trying to squeeze into apartment parking spots, which
wasn't good, but I was making some serious cheddar cheese.

I was also eating my fair share of leftover cheddar cheese because that's what happens to orders that don't get picked up.

Things were looking up in life, although my diet was still garbage. My love for movies remained, and I spent pretty much any downtime at the theater. I was that guy who went to a 1pm matinee showing of *The Amazing Spider-Man 2* and bought two Slurpees and two hot dogs. And then did it again the next day.

In my defense, I absolutely love that movie.

Caught up in the fact that I actually had a job, writing gigs on the side and a renewed lease on life, my weight slipped through the cracks, and I ballooned to more than 200 pounds by the end of the year.

My sports writing had started to get the attention of some important people, and in August I got a job at CBS Radio as a promotions assistant. If you're unsure of what that is, don't worry, I still am too.

Ironically, I had gotten a job at the same place a couple years earlier as an intern for the radio show *G-Bag Nation*. But that internship was tied to school credit, and when I dropped out, well, goodbye internship.

For the first time in my four (or five?) jobs, I left on good terms. I said goodbye to Domino's and glorious leftovers and went to work at CBS Radio. As a promotions assistant, I made below the minimum wage. It was essentially a paid internship where I did anything and everything that was asked of the radio show hosts in the name of eventually moving up.

This meant long days on the set of radio shows, which didn't sound too bad in theory. I quickly discovered that I was basically a henchman, arriving hours early to shows to set up and staying well after to take down. After a morning show for the sports crew, I'd get a few hours before doing a night show for the music team.

I took the job to get an "in" to the journalism industry, as most everyone in the position did. The job came with the stipulation that we would work our way up, but it became evident pretty quickly that that wasn't going to happen.

I was basically an indentured servant. I worked almost the whole day, every day, got paid like $5 an hour and was mostly treated like garbage. On my first day, I was working a promotional event at a car dealership for the sports station 105.3 The Fan, and somewhere around hour five, I got in trouble with a sales rep for taking a quick break to sit down.

On my second day, I stood on the corner holding a sign for two hours advertising our music station. I was *that guy* doing the twirls and the spins and all that jazz.

As if sitting down was bad enough, about a month later I was working an event for the same sports station at the Gaylord Texan palace in Grapevine. After setting up for a few hours, my back was killing me, and all I wanted was to take a quick seat. But I wasn't going to chance it. However, this time I was reprimanded for getting a glass of water.

The biggest selling point of the job was that I got to go to Dallas Cowboys games. After working about five hours of pregame by manning an inflatable, I did indeed get to watch the game from the field-level club. That was cool, although I was right behind the visiting team's bench and couldn't see any of the game.

Since I could only see the game via the gigantic scoreboard screen, I was basically watching it on TV. I wondered why none of the other employees were excited about staying for the game. I thought that was the cool part of the job!

Two hours after the game ended, I was still in traffic driving the station van back to the office, and I finally understood why nobody stayed. The van was old, smelly and full of equipment that was blocking the rearview window. I'm just glad I made it back! (Although I did bump the van's antenna on the parking garage entrance sign.)

Repairing the antenna ended up being of no consequence, rather it was sitting down and drinking water that got me in trouble on the job. When I told my supervisor, the lovely Anne, that I wanted to quit, she didn't sound surprised. Apparently, I was just another hopeful, aspiring worker who fell for the same sales pitch. In their defense, it's a good system for finding low-cost labor and hard-working people.

The most fun I had at this job, which I took to break into the sports industry, had nothing to do with sports. One of the channels under the CBS Radio umbrella was KVIL, a pop music radio station. I worked several events for this wing of the company and got to actually talk while behind the promotions table – to my co-workers, to customers, just talk. And I could even sit and take a water break. Everybody was there to do their job, but it didn't feel like military school.

The sports people took themselves way too seriously. The music people had a blast. The vibe was completely different, but I was still bummed out that the reason I went to work there ended up being the reason I wanted to leave.

I found the positives and started to work almost exclusively for the music station. My hours started to make more sense; I was no longer working two-a-days, getting off at 3am and eating at the next-door McDonald's for dinner while I drove home on the tollway with my eyes half shut. I seriously don't know how I made it home some days.

Still, I really did not like this job, so I started looking for a new one. It didn't happen for a few months, but in the meantime, I had another Marvel-inspired emotional awakening.

*****

Back in April, my opening-night experience at *Captain America: The Winter Soldier* had really stuck with me. It was an incredible feeling that I wanted to recapture. I hadn't felt that genuine stroke of happiness since George W. Bush was in office. Not because he was the president; I'm just marking the time.

I had a similar experience with *The Amazing Spider-Man 2* in May, as I mentioned above. I even saw it with Pierce for old times' sake, rekindling decade-old memories from *Spider-Man 2* in 2004.

Talking about movies, 2014 was a heck of a year. Along with the Cap and Spidey sequels, we had another great sequel, *Dawn of the Planet of the Apes*. Also, *John Wick*, *Boyhood*, *Nightcrawler*, *Big Hero 6* and even the X-Men franchise got something right with *Days of Future Past*!

But it was Marvel Studios' second picture of the year that had nearly as big of an impact on me as the first one four months earlier.

On the eve of August, *Guardians of the Galaxy* came out. Now, *Guardians* wasn't just a great film – it was a film that made you feel good about life. That's a typical goal in entertainment, but it doesn't happen more often than it does. This movie was a feel-good blockbuster spectacle that nobody saw coming.

The star of the film, Chris Pratt, also inspired me. Pratt went from overweight schlub to sexy protagonist to portray Peter Quill, aka Star-Lord. Now, my goal wasn't to become sexy or a protagonist, but seeing him go through this change gave me confidence to do the same.

This feeling didn't manifest until a few months later, when I pulled my mom aside on our December Mexico trip and told her I wanted to lose weight, for real this time. But the idea was planted pretty firmly in my head when I saw what Pratt had done for the role.

Another motivational moment in the waning months of 2014 happened at a Mavericks game against the Utah Jazz. The Jazz had become my favorite team along with the Mavs for a few reasons.

They had two of my favorite players at the same time: Devin Harris and Gordon Hayward. They had a baby blue alternate jersey. They have a loyal, passionate fan base. And lastly, I had really started to take a liking to small-market teams across all sports. Particularly the Jazz, the Miami Marlins and a trio of NFL teams: the Miami Dolphins, Jacksonville Jaguars and the San Diego-turned-Los Angeles Chargers.

All these various franchises joined my eclectic rooting interests that included the Dallas teams, the Giants and the Astros. I know it's considered sacrilege to be a fan of so many teams, and I was told as much many times, but after so passionately rooting for certain teams growing up, I was turning into more of a fan of the game, not just individual teams.

Anyway, at the Mavericks and Jazz game, I got a picture and autograph from Hayward. I also asked him for a wristband he was wearing, as I did with many athletes, which resulted in a closet full of old, sweaty, game-worn gear. He said he wanted to wear it for the game but to ask him after.

That usually means "no," but sure enough, after the game, he tossed me his wristband. The gray bracelet reads, "Eyes Up, Do The Work," in yellow letters, and this small little gesture, this wristband he tossed me six and a half years ago as of the moment I type this, has stuck with me.

I'm still wearing it today, and the words on it, accompanied with Hayward's act of kindness, served as further motivation to improve myself. In times of doubt, and we all have them, I found those five simple words both reassuring and inspiring.

Again – people need heroes. Becoming a pro athlete or a superhero is unfortunately out of the question (unless I go the *Kick-Ass* route), but getting back in shape was a task that even a regular human like myself could easily accomplish.

Eyes up, do the work.

***

The year 2014 had so much going on, and although I hit my lowest point in those 365 days, I actually look back on it and see it not as a year of tragedy, but a year of hope. I got knocked down, but I got up with a renewed sense of purpose, even if it took a few months to kick in.

I worked. I watched a lot of movies, and I did something else that was very important. For the first time since maybe 2010 or 2011, I reached out to some old friends.

When I was unwell, I pretty much cut myself off from the world. My old friends made new ones, and I was a Yoda-like hermit, wasting away at home and doing nothing with my life. (No offense, Yoda.)

But in 2014, I got back in touch with Jake and another friend, Brian, who I was extremely close with in elementary school but had fallen out of touch with. We spent the summer and fall of 2014 reconnecting over Mavericks games, Cowboys games and a whole bunch of movies.

Nine years earlier, Jake had introduced me to *Star Wars*. Now, I was introducing him to the Marvel Cinematic Universe. The circle of life is a beautiful thing.

(Which reminds me, *The Lion King* – one of the greatest films of all time.)

CHAPTER 20

2015 – THE COMEBACK KID

Things were definitely looking up, and for the first time in a long time, I felt optimistic about the future. Rather than my usual resignation that "this is just the way it is" for me, I thought I could really do something with my life.

OCD was still a factor, and it always will be, but my best and only hope was to learn to make the most of my situation – to live with the disease and not let it hold me back.

To this day, my OCD is still a problem. Every second of every single day, my mind is moving at a speed with which I can't keep up, full of thoughts that have the sole purpose of causing me anxiety and stress.

It's a constant battle, but as 2015 began, it was one I finally felt like I could fight. I guess it took me nine years to raise an army.

While on our family trip in Mexico, my parents heard something from me they had been wanting to hear for years. I was ready to quit being a baby (a little harsh but, hey, it's me I'm talking about), get off my ass (harsh again, but still me) and lose the weight that I had been steadily putting on for the last several years.

At that point, I had peaked at 206 pounds. For all the things improving in my life, this was something still holding me back. A key to improving my depression and loneliness and instilling me with some confidence would be to shed this excess weight.

My mom, being the resourceful wizard she is, found a place literally up the street called Utopia Food & Fitness. As it says in its name, Utopia is a place of healthy food and a workout gym, where they arm you with a very specific and carefully outlined diet plan to get you back on the good side of life.

My mom was skinny then, skinny now, and has always been skinny, but being the team player she is, she went on the Utopia diet and workout plan with me.

Beyond tired of the shape I was in, I jumped into the Utopia plan with enthusiasm and saw very quick results.

Utopia's plan is built around a daily calorie count, with breakfast, lunch, dinner and a snack provided by their kitchen. For the first time in a long time, I was eating breakfast. It's the most important meal of the day, people! Your doctor is telling the truth!

The workout plan for Utopia is almost impossible to believe and/or too good to be true. Along with the restricted calorie plan, I was only required to work out twice a week for about 20 minutes.

If you think it sounds like a scam, I don't blame you. But this is literally the program. Eat their food and workout at their gym twice a week for not even an hour total.

I was shedding weight in no time. Less than a week in, I was under 200 pounds. A month later, I weighed in at under 190. By summer, I was around 170, and I hit 150 by the end of the year. Today, I am about 140 pounds and have never put the weight back on.

As I write this, my sister is on their program for wedding prep, several of her friends are on it, and my mom still gets the food. This isn't a paid endorsement for Utopia, but I'm not above book-deal sponsorships.

Looking like my older self brought a new confidence to my life. Or should I say, it brought confidence to my life for the first time in a long time. I've never been a very confident person, and my illness took any sort of childhood swagger I'd had and cast it aside. But now, I was feeling like I mattered, and I could actually look myself in the mirror without feeling shame.

Soon after I started Utopia, I found another job. That brought a merciful end to the CBS Radio gig, and with help of some of my online sports connections, I started hosting my own radio show.

Sports journalism, like most things, is all about networking, and I had made some new friends through Twitter who had an imprint on the local scene, including Michael Allardyce and Brian Cuban, who hosted their own radio show. After filling in for Cuban for an episode, I got in touch with Jamie Kelly, who asked me to appear as a guest on her radio show, which was produced from a restaurant in Carrollton for the radio station KTSR.

Before long, they asked me to host my own show. I teamed up with the talented duo of Kirk Jones and Sarah Powers, and twice a week we hosted a sports and entertainment show called *The Young Guns*, named for a rival team my youth baseball team beat in one of the most impressive wins of my career. Pierce and another friend, Jackson, will remember.

We had a blast. All three of us were big fans of the radio station The Ticket, although one of our benefactors, Mike Fisher, was a frequent guest of my former home radio station, The Fan. We patterned our show after the award-winning, critically acclaimed programs on The Ticket like *Dunham and Miller* and *BaD Radio*.

It was a mix of sports, movies, TV, pop culture and anything we wanted. Kelly, our boss, gave us free reign to do the show as we pleased. It was a glimpse into a life and career I could see myself doing, doing well and enjoying. The job at CBS came with the hope of breaking in, but here I actually got to do real journalism, not just sleep in the front seat of a van between eight-hour shifts.

As great as this gig was, it was just twice a week and wasn't a reliable source of income. A few weeks earlier, I remember driving home from the CBS job and brainstorming possible jobs I could work in tandem with this one.

After holding multiple jobs I didn't like, but also realizing beggars can't be choosers, I was nevertheless committed to the idea of doing something I *wanted* to do, but also something I could put on my résumé like the KTSR role.

Somewhere in the daily traffic grind of the Dallas North Tollway, I think between Wycliff Avenue and Royal Lane, it hit me.

***

Since I was very young, I always loved the stadium public-address announcers at sporting events. Granted, they're not all great, but I was absolutely spoiled growing up with the legendary Chuck Morgan behind the mic at Texas Rangers games, and he's still there to this day.

If there's a heaven, I believe I'll be greeted at the pearly gates with Chuck's famous pregame introduction.

"IT IS BASEBALL TIME IN TEXAS!"

His voice, and just the way he pauses so majestically between each of those six words – it's enough to bring me to tears.

On the basketball front, the Dallas Mavericks had the iconic "Humble" Billy Hayes, famous for his elongated free throw shot primer: "Steve Nash will have twoooooooooooooooooooooo…

… shots.

Hayes retired from his post in 2010, and Sean Heath, a kindhearted man who I would end up becoming friends with over the years, stepped into the role. His coup de grâce, at least in my opinion, is pronouncing the great Dirk Nowitzki's name with an overlong "Dirrrrrrrrrrrrr… k."

Talking with him years later, he told me he got the idea from a license plate. That's epic.

As a kid, when I would play my sports video games, I took on the role of either the play-by-play announcer or the PA announcer. I also admired two men in the former field, the Mavericks' Mark Followill and the Rangers' Josh Lewin. Followill became a friend and a mentor to me when I got older and more serious about a job in sports.

After games, when fans would clamor for the attention of players, coaches or whomever, I would always go down and say hi to the broadcasters and announcers. It became a sort of ritual, a word I don't use lightly.

At home, I loved taking on this role while I played video games or played outside.

When I played basketball on the hoop at my house, I would simulate real-life games. I was all the players, passing the ball around the painted concrete to myself, shooting as one player, rebounding as another, and I would narrate it all from the position of play-by-play announcer, color commentator and PA announcer.

It was a lot. But I was a kid obsessed.

The most memorable moment in all of my childhood broadcasting was probably when I was announcing my video games from the den, and my sister came storming in from her room next door.

"Who are you talking to? I'm trying to study!"

I didn't have a good answer because I was talking to myself. But who doesn't love those brother-sister bonding moments?

A future as a PA announcer is extremely rare, but I absolutely loved it. So, on that drive home, I reached out to one of my rec-center friends who was currently on the varsity baseball team at my alma mater, Plano West Senior High School.

I asked him if they had an announcer for home games, and he said it was currently one of the team dads who was only doing it to help.

He put me in touch with the head coach, Coach Clark. Though I never played baseball for him after sports left my equation following tenth-grade basketball, he was my PE teacher in middle school, and he remembered me. Plus, some people I knew from high school had played for him back in 2013. One of them, Billy McKinney, even went pro as a first-round draft pick. He was drafted while I was in Rome, to shed some light on that unholy trip. Another player, Ryan McAfee, did not go pro, but he's one of my friends to this day, so here's a shoutout.

Coach Clark and I quickly reconnected over our mutual friends and, within minutes of seeing him again for the first time in years, he offered me the job as the team's stadium announcer.

So, by February 2015, I had two new jobs and was down about 15 pounds. Being productive felt great! I could definitely get used to it.

I continued to write, and I wrote a lot. I purchased a website domain name, aptly titled asherfeltman.com, and my cousin designed a spiffy Squarespace setup for me. This became the home site of all my work, from writing to radio to anything in between.

I was doing so much better, but the idea of downtime still gave me goosebumps. Any moment of calm made me so anxious that I would fill it with worry. Aside from ERP, the best treatment for my smorgasbord of symptoms has always been to stay busy. Like a lot of other normal warm-blooded humans, I get very antsy when I have nothing to do.

Especially since the times when I wasn't busy painfully reminded me of what my life had been for so long. I was scared of these moments and didn't want my mind to have a chance to wander.

I stayed busy, and I mostly did so by writing. I also transformed my fantasy baseball and basketball leagues into a full beast of expanded keeper leagues, with minor leaguers and G Leaguers, contracts and a whole bunch of other stuff that isn't worth explaining.

My commitment to staying occupied was neurotic and obsessive. But the latter applied to anything I did, for better and worse.

I had the first of two nasal septum surgeries in 2015, and while I won't go into that much more, my biggest takeaway from the experience was how quickly my obsessive thoughts started coming back to me once I woke up from the anesthesia. That was a disappointing development. But those unconscious moments were nice.

Still, writing was my biggest fix, and I started to get paid for it through a website called *Minor League Ball*. Owned and operated by the famous prospect guru John Sickels, I started to collect compensation for my baseball writing and became an official, credentialed member of the press for minor league baseball games.

These minor league baseball games just so happened to be at my old stomping grounds, the Dr. Pepper Ballpark, home of the Frisco RoughRiders.

Despite my unceremonious exit back in 2011, this was still a second home to me. I still met up with Alex there every summer, when he would visit with his dad from Oklahoma. As Alex got older, I got more involved with his life.

Even though we only saw each other once a year, he really did feel like the younger brother I never had. Seeing him was a treat, and our late nights at the ballpark were a tradition that returned in 2015, since I was healthy and available.

We never really talked about where I had been or what had happened. He was still a kid, and the world was a happy place of hope and dreams. Being back together again felt like we hadn't missed any time.

Returning to the home of the RoughRiders, I got in touch with Chuck Greenberg, the owner of the team as of a few years prior. He played in the same softball league as me, and in the middle of saying hi to each other at a game, he mentioned to me that they needed some help in the clubhouse manager/batboy department.

Knowing I used to work there, and not concerned with the sketchy way things ended with previous management, he offered me the same batboy position I used to hold, plus added responsibilities as an assistant clubhouse manager.

I told him I was honored but had reservations because of the way things used to be in that area. He said it was new management, new people and a new culture. He was right on all counts, and I slid back into the job like no time had passed.

My revolving door of jobs all of a sudden became a catalog of employment. I was working my radio show and the Plano West job, getting paid to write for the first time and now was back with the RoughRiders.

In a weird way, it was like my life would have gone this direction if I hadn't gotten sick. Things were happening that I'd always planned; there was just a nine-or-ten-year "pause" that had kept me from moving forward.

Now, I was moving and moving fast.

CHAPTER 21

2016 – REEL LIFE

In hindsight, I feel like my life has been a movie. Make that multiple movies. It has taken on many forms and many genres. I almost feel like Steven Spielberg could be directing it. Trust me, I'm not saying my life is some grand spectacle like *Jurassic Park* or *Indiana Jones*. It's not a thought-provoking epic like *Schindler's List* or *Saving Private Ryan*.

Maybe it's *E.T. the Extra-Terrestrial*, but that's not the point I'm trying to make.

The celebrated filmmaker Spielberg is famous for his unpredictability as an artist. There is no rhyme or reason to the movies he makes. He can make *The Post* and then turn around and do *Ready Player One*, and nobody bats an eye.

So, when I say I think he could be secretly directing my life, I mean my life from 2015 and on. Before that, my movie was in development hell. But since 2015, I've worn many, many hats.

I believe that life, ultimately, is about experimentation. We are on this Earth to find our purpose. That comes with experimentation.

Discovering things. Trying new things. Trying and failing. Trying something else. At least for me, life is all about finding where we fit.

This is why we learn all those subjects in elementary, middle and high school and in college. Over and over. Us humans are not so complicated. We just want to find out where we fit in in this thing called life.

These discoveries usually happen in our youth, in our formative years. Childhood, the teenage years and early adulthood are times for self-discovery. For me, I never had that opportunity.

It is my biggest regret.

My life got put on pause at age 12. My teenage years were not what I wanted them to be. I didn't get to stick with school sports or club sports as planned. My friendships disappeared. Those fun sleepovers and pool parties and awkward dates with girls I said two words to in the hall, they were no more. Of all that I have lost, I wish I could have continued to make those memories.

I was never the student I could have been. My grades were not representative of my intellect. I switched schools and then switched again. I wasn't meant to have a college experience like my friends and family had.

I believe that's why I get along with kids and young adults so well. I never experienced what they get to experience – that truly wonderful, hopeful, optimistic time of your life. I never had that, so perhaps I live vicariously through young people. At the very least, I want them to appreciate the moments and not take them away from them as this world tends to do.

You only get one life, and I missed too much of mine. I wrestle with that fact every day, and I refuse to let it cripple my well-being, but it's a tough pill to swallow.

In 2016 I had finally emerged from a decade-long slumber. I lost so, so, so much time and I wanted to get it back. I didn't have a time machine, but I did have time.

I had time to experiment. Finally. To try different things and see what I wanted out of life. It felt good to be searching, to do things I *wanted* to do!

All at once, I was finally experiencing the childhood that I had thought was lost forever. I was a young adult, but I was going through an accelerated childhood and discovering things about myself and life that I never got the proper chance to.

Much of this progress started in 2015, but when 2016 started, I did a bit of reshuffling on the job front.

I had really, really gotten into movies and wanted to give that industry another shot. I applied at Cinemark, whose headquarters are actually down the street from my parents' home, and I got a job at the original flagship location in Plano, Texas.

At the end of February 2016, I was working four jobs: Cinemark, the RoughRiders, Plano West and Lifetime Fitness. The job at Lifetime was low pay but came with a free membership. All I did was show up once a week, keep score for the basketball league and then write postgame articles for the league's Facebook site. It was easy, on the side and another thing I enjoyed.

I remember during this time that I would tell my mom or dad that I was headed for work, and they would half-jokingly ask, "Which work?"

This was a particularly great time for me. I stayed busy, just as I wanted. I was working – and working a lot – especially at Cinemark. Most of the theater employees were high school or college kids, so I was able to work the closing hours until about 1 or 2 in the morning.

This mostly meant walking around an empty building and making sure nobody had fallen asleep at a midnight showing of *Suicide Squad* (which would be totally understandable).

Some days, I would finish a Cinemark shift at 2am, work another in the afternoon, then go to Frisco for my RoughRiders job the following evening. It was a lot, but as I said, this was what I wanted. I had never been so happy to be so busy.

I was so busy, in fact, that I'd return home from work in the early morning hours and still stay up to play video games or watch TV. I found any time I could to experience the joys that had eluded me for so many years.

I got into a real rhythm with all my jobs. Cinemark was year-round, Plano West was from February to May, the RoughRiders was March to September, and Lifetime fell on Thursdays.

In a twist that will surprise no one, the biggest perk of working at a movie theater was free movies. Jake was in town for the summer after wrapping up college, and I also reconnected with Brett, a friend from high school, and became good friends with Ben, a Plano West baseball player, as we bonded over our mutual love of *Star Wars* and especially Spider-Man.

My love for movies went from passion to obsession in the summer of 2016. It was a fantastic year for film, blockbuster and indie alike. Movies like *Captain America: Civil War, Rogue One: A Star Wars Story, Sing Street, Eddie the Eagle* and *Doctor Strange* encouraged me to start charting my all-time favorite films, a list that still exists today and recent eclipsed 700 movies.

Available by request for an unlimited time.

***

The steps I took in 2016 will forever define me. Although 2015 may have been the year I decided to turn my life around, 2016 is when I did it. I started to dream again – and dream big. For years, I thought the best I could do was just survive in a state of complacency. Now, I was believing in myself for the first time, and it felt good.

The time I lost was time I could have built up a résumé, but now I was doing that in hyper-speed like the Millennium Falcon escaping the Empire. I felt like I was living in fast-forward, every day a sprint, but it felt right.

As I hit summer in 2016, I started to see Dr. Abel twice a month, down from three times, which represented a big step in my OCD journey. I was becoming more self-sufficient, even if I had a long way to go at age 23.

My obsessions, compulsions and symptoms were down across the board. They were still there, and I was still an expert at disguising them at critical moments, like when the home plate umpire ran out of baseballs and needed a refill, or when theater 12 was ready to be cleaned.

After several months of working my four-job rotation, a lightbulb went off in my head that really signified that I was thinking about the future.

I hadn't even thought about school in a couple years, but every time I contemplated my future, my education was the thing I kept coming back to.

I wanted to do more with the RoughRiders than work in the clubhouse. I was writing for professional publications, but I wanted to work directly for the club in a more professional capacity. Despite credentials that were piling up, my lack of a college degree was a glaring omission from my portfolio.

I will admit that in the sports journalism industry, a college degree is not a requirement, and it is not at all unusual to get a job in the business without one. A part of me was banking on this, but the other part knew the benefits of finishing school.

Not only that, but my dad always told me how much he wanted me to go to college. To have the, in his words, "college experience." At 23 and with just a semester under my belt, I was never going to go to a four-year school and party my heart out like he, my sister, Jake and Brian did at the University of Texas. Or my brother Alec at the University of Arizona. Or my mom at Tulane.

Although partying for my mom was probably drinking a diet coke, snacking on pretzels and studying until the morning light.

Nevertheless, it was something that weighed on me. No matter what I did, whether I even needed a degree or not, I thought it would be a great accomplishment and something to be proud of if I could come all the way back from where I was and finish school.

With so much work on my plate, that fall I signed up for a local learning course through Collin College. It was my way of easing back in, but it wasn't for credit, and it wasn't really college.

I wasn't ready to give up my work, especially when I caught my biggest break yet in September.

With baseball season ending, my plate was emptying a bit, but basketball season was coming into view. My writing was predominantly about baseball, but I still occasionally contributed basketball content, and my passion for the game remained.

Literally across the street from the Minor League Baseball RoughRiders are the G League (formerly D-League) Texas Legends, the minor league basketball affiliate of the Dallas Mavericks.

I was referred to a position with the Legends by a family friend and connection in the sports world, Jared Sandler, who had taken over as the TV voice of the Legends. Jared always said in polite protest to my many thank-yous, "I only opened the door."

Before long, I was interviewing with Legends' President and General Manager Malcolm Farmer, who offered me the position as the team's leading staff writer. I had worked with the RoughRiders for over five years, but this was my biggest, most credible and most legitimate break in the sports journalism industry.

I essentially became a full-time reporter, covering anything and everything the Legends did. I was so graciously welcomed by experienced basketball minds like Farmer, Donnie Nelson, Del Harris, Bob MacKinnon and Spud Webb.

Coincidentally, I had worked at a Texas Legends event years earlier. My friend T.J.'s mom, Nancy Lieberman, was the first coach the organization had. That, and she's the greatest women's basketball player of all time.

My first assignment was the annual open tryout that the Legends hold before every season. Then, I was at the team's draft party. Then media day, practices, all the games, and even a road trip. I've worked a lot of jobs, but the work environment and culture at the Texas Legends was one of true respect, comfort and teamwork – something you just don't see a whole lot of in the workplace (or world) anymore.

I mean, really, I have to mention the incredibly wonderful Britney Wynn, the Vice President of Community & Media Relations for the team. Talk about someone having your back. Wynn was everywhere and anywhere I needed when I was with the Legends, and having her by my side every day was the best part of that job.

For example, Cinemark was a bit of a mess. What do you expect from a place where most of the employees are teenagers? But my patience was wearing thin. I soon felt overqualified to be cleaning theaters and having to yell at kids to get off their butts and work.

That job was almost always fun. I love movies, I love being around people, and I got to mix those together being an usher at Cinemark. I even got a wave from the one and only Taron Egerton at an *Eddie the Eagle* press event the theater held. Feather placed firmly in the cap.

But after a particularly long day in September, I really lost my patience with a trio of young employees and said some things I shouldn't have. The next day, I was fired from Cinemark after seven months there. And then, a week later, I was offered a managerial position at a different Cinemark.

I took this job and reported to my first Frisco shift, but then I realized that this chapter of my life had passed. It was time to put the movie industry behind me, save for pursuing a late-blooming, Liam Neeson-esque Hollywood career in my twilight years.

Things got a little slower in the fall, and I even did some catering through a family friend's barbeque business, which I hated and was terrible at, but it made me good money. I also continued to write for the Legends, which I loved and was good at, but it made me less money.

The highlight of my Legends career came almost immediately. I wrote a feature story on the truly wonderful human being that is Quincy Acy, who had played for the Legends before joining the Brooklyn Nets, and that story made it onto SportsCenter.

ESPN's Scott Van Pelt read an excerpt from my story on the air, attributing it to me on live TV, and the Legends front office filmed it for me. I hold this memory and accomplishment close to my heart, despite eventually changing my career plans down the line.

I have to say, that night, when my name was said on national television, I heard from a lot of people I hadn't heard from in a long time. And haven't heard from since. Such is the spotlight!

Putting a bow on 2016 is difficult, because the two-year stretch of 2015 and 2016 was the turning point in my life. For how far I had fallen, how low I had sunk, I had climbed out to a point where I was in position to really do something with this life.

That meant a lot to me, but it meant even more to me that I could reward the faith that people had put and kept in me for the last ten years.

CHAPTER 22

2017, PART 1 – COLLEGE, PART 2

When I started to think about re-enrolling in college, I got a look at my original transcripts from 2012-2013. To say the least, they weren't pretty. I had accumulated three total credits, two "F's" and a "C."

In the words of Obi-Wan Kenobi after Jango Fett lassoed him together in *Attack of the Clones*, "Not good." I know the circumstances were rough, but the first thing on the agenda was to turn those grades into a more respectable number, and then reboot from there.

Because of my rocky first foray into higher education, I was actually on academic probation. I went back to Collin College in Plano to retake these courses and set my path on a new trajectory, which is just what I did.

Not to let myself off the hook, but I don't even count my first attempt at college as a real one. Even still, those grades were on my record, and I was determined to wipe them out, like Palpatine attempted to do to the Gungan army in *The Phantom Menace*.

(You thought the *Star Wars* references were over?)

Before it all went sideways in 2006, I was a great student. I know we're talking about elementary school, but I've always been an extremely disciplined person and very particular about everything I do.

As a kid, I was obsessively detailed, a foreboding precursor to what was to come, but it nonetheless made me a very organized, careful and responsible learner.

These habits came back to me all at once during my second semester of college. I took three classes for a total of nine credit hours – a small, manageable load to get me back in the swing of things – but there was also another Feltman family trip that played a factor.

In 2017, my accomplished sister finished med school at the University of Texas Health Science Center at San Antonio. A top student at the University of Texas, she held the same status at UTSA and is without a doubt the smartest Feltman child. (Sorry Alec – I know you agree.)

To celebrate her accomplishment, our family took a trip to South Africa. Family trips, especially across the Atlantic Ocean, had been a sore spot for me in the past, but outside of the long flight that shook my nerves, I was excited to go to Africa and, at the very least, see the animals on a safari or perhaps find a secret entrance to Wakanda.

Feltman vacations always seem to have some sort of baggage attached, but the Africa trip takes the cake. Our connecting flight from Dallas to Atlanta was delayed, and we missed our connecting flight from Atlanta to Johannesburg by literal seconds.

After landing, we sprinted through the airport just to have the boarding doors shut on us as we approached. I get it, regulations are regulations, but it was a bummer. A sweaty bummer.

So, we spent a night in Atlanta instead of seeing Victoria Falls. At least I got to see the very first Chick-Fil-A. It was their pleasure.

I navigated my return to school around the trip, and a crazy trip it was. I finished the semester with three As, setting a new standard for myself as a student and resuming my education with a bang.

In the summers of 2017, 2018 and 2019, I would take as many summer school classes as possible. I was glad to be back in school, but that didn't mean I wanted to take my time. For all I had been through, I considered myself way behind schedule.

I wanted to catch up to life, if you will, but my family and friends urged me to slow down and try and enjoy the belated ride.

With my return to school, I lightened up on the work front. I continued to work for Plano West and the Legends, but I left my post at Lifetime and departed the RoughRiders with another baseball position coming into play.

That summer, I received a message from my very first clubhouse manager with the RoughRiders. He heard I was back in the batboy game (which sounds cooler than it really is) and reached out about a position with the Texas Rangers, where he now ran the home clubhouse.

In a matter of days, I was interviewing for a position in the visiting clubhouse. I thought it was a batboy position like what I did with the RoughRiders: show up a few hours before the game, set up, work the game, tear down and stay a few hours after to prepare for the following gameday.

Well, the RoughRiders are a Double-A Minor League team. The Rangers are "The Show," and everything is bigger there.

I immediately sensed this was a different beast when my first shift *started* at midnight. I thought, "Okay, that's late, but I'll be out of there by 4 or 5am." After loading the departing Miami Marlins bags on their team bus, we waited to receive the bags for the incoming Baltimore Orioles.

I didn't get home until about 11am and then drove to class at 1pm. I expected different things at the big-league level, but this was crazy. With respect to big-league clubhouse attendants, I couldn't possibly do what they do. But this was an opportunity I didn't want to let go of… until my sports bubble finally burst.

***

As you age, you tend to realize the world around you isn't as innocent and fun as it was when you were a kid. You grow up and take your place in the world and realize that everything around you isn't the sandbox you once played in.

I'm not saying it's all doom and gloom and the wonder is gone, because that's not completely true. However, my childhood as a sports fan was absolutely seen through rose-tinted glasses and a pocket full of optimistic sunshine.

As I got older, I quickly realized that the sports industry, not unlike any other industry, is all about money. What in life isn't? It's a sucky lesson to learn, but it arrives as inevitably as Thanos does at the onset of *Avengers: Infinity War.*

I especially noticed this as I began to work in the sports industry. Not just writing for websites, but actually covering sporting events, interviewing owners, managers, coaches and players, and physically witnessing the insane amount of moving *human* parts that make up an organization.

It's a lesson any rational person would eventually learn, but it was especially crushing for me, as sports were my escape as a kid. Now, that escape has become movies and entertainment, and Lord knows I never want to see the inside of that industry.

My naive ideologies were hard to preserve, even working in first-class organizations like the Legends or the Rangers. It's not where I worked, but what I *saw* and what I *did* with the Rangers that officially burst my sports bubble.

My hours with the Rangers were nearly 24-hour shifts when the team was at home. "Clubbies" are completely off when the team is on the road, which provides some balance. But when the team is playing at home, you're at the park all day, every day.

That wasn't the primary issue, but rather it was the type of tasks I was to perform as a Major League Baseball clubhouse assistant. On my second day (and first non-midnight shift), my big task was to go to the corner drugstore and buy chewing tobacco for one of the Orioles pitchers.

I've never used the stuff, and purchasing it was one of the sketchiest things I've ever done. (I don't live very dangerously.) Upon returning to the park, I gave the chew to the head clubbie, who gave it to the pitcher, who gave the clubbie the money, who then gave it to me. It was just odd.

I also learned why we all want to be some sort of famous. Whether it's a professional athlete, Hollywood actor, rich business mogul… whatever it is, I saw first-hand why that life is so coveted.

Achieving any of those lines of work is difficult, and pretty much everyone involved has earned their stripes, but holy cow, Batman, do they live like kings! An MLB clubhouse is a five-star resort in every way. The coffee bar alone was insane. And I proceeded to make coffee for the Orioles bullpen before that night's game. Hey, sitting through nine innings night after night can be a grind!

What really blew me away more than anything was the service. I get that we were there to be of assistance. It's literally in the job title. But working in a baseball clubhouse should be fun, as it was in Frisco. Working with the Rangers, I was on pins and needles at all times of the day. Any down moment needed to be filled, whether it was scrubbing cleats, restocking the glamorous coffee bar, or the coup de grâce, picking up shower towels designed specifically for the, uh, groin area.

Yes, the players had shower towels specifically for their (base)balls. I was in charge of picking those up when most of them just tossed them aside instead of hitting the bottom of the bin. This was my least favorite part of the job, second to the sense of dread everyone seemed to feel for the members of the team. Those towels were really small, too, so I was always getting a fistful of regret.

The tips were good, but the payoff was not. Nobody seemed to be enjoying themselves. I remember on the day the Orioles came in, one of my superiors said to stay way, way, way out of the way of one of Baltimore's coaches.

"Don't go near him," he said. "Just don't."

For the record, I thought he was just fine. Baseball coaches tend to wear a permanent scowl, but underneath their rugged exterior, you might find a kind man willing to shoot the breeze. You might.

I knew there were egos in the business, but it wasn't a joyful working environment. I understood the level of stardom and fame we were dealing with, but when I was picking up the towel that someone just wiped their butt with, I felt like I should have at least enjoyed myself every now and then.

And that I did, especially when game time approached. That was the job I signed up for after all, and it was absolutely thrilling.

A few hours before the game, after getting all the dugout supplies set up – the water coolers, Gatorade, bubble gum, sunflower seeds, medical equipment, player equipment, etc. – I got to help shag batting practice.

The highlight of my time at that job was in batting practice, which recalled memories of years earlier when I would spend that time in Frisco with Martín Pérez, Marcus Lemon and the gang.

One day in Frisco, way back when, a bird went to the bathroom on me, and Pérez absolutely loved that in the kindest way possible that somebody can love that.

During batting practice, pitchers are doing most of the shagging. They aren't in any of the hitting groups, so they are always in the field catching, and doing this day after day means looking for ways to pass the time.

Orioles pitcher Ubaldo Jiménez did this by throwing me absolutely filthy cutters. I missed several before I finally started to keep up with the 90-plus MPH moving action on his throws.

He got a kick out of this, and he spent roughly 90 minutes challenging me with his nastiest stuff. When the Orioles departed days later, Jiménez sought me out personally and handed me a $100 bill.

Now, Jiménez was playing on a four-year, $50 million contract, and made north of $65 million in his career, so I think he ended up okay. Still, that experience and that gesture are a highlight of my time working in the majors.

During my short tenure with the Rangers, I also got to see Hall of Famer Adrián Beltré collect his 3,000th career hit up close. That was quite the experience, to say the least.

The whole thing was a bit surreal. Being on the field, being a part of a big-league game, seeing everything that goes into the day-to-day operations, even if it was from a keyhole perspective, was a lot. Unfortunately, the dwindling passion I had for sports was starting to drain, and this experience couldn't reverse it.

My fluttering feelings for the industry started to leak into my writing. Whereas writing used to be something I looked forward to and had a devout passion for, it now felt more like a chore. Instead of planning my day around writing time, I no longer wanted to set aside that time, and though I did not truly let it affect my work, I felt both the quality and my interest begin to waver.

I wasn't as active on sports social media, whether for promoting my work or engaging in whatever storylines the fans were following. In the current sports journalism climate, it pays to be involved on social media, and I was losing my presence there as well as my readers.

No longer were my tweets about the Mavericks, Rangers or even sports in general. Instead, if and when I tweeted, it was more about life, my own musings, movies, music or other things I was taking an increased interest in over what had been the primary focus of my world for almost 25 years… sports.

It was a personality shift, and it was happening all at once without me fully realizing it.

CHAPTER 23

2017, PART 2 – CAP'S LIST

My first semester back at college was a success. After acing two more classes in summer school, my academic probation was lifted. While I was experiencing success as a student, I still craved a social life.

Collin College is not billed as a community college, but it operates in that spirit. There are multiple campuses, and I spent the spring at the Plano campus. There are some who live on campus at nearby apartments, but it is largely a commuter school, and that was how it was for me.

You don't go to Collin for the typical college life, and that's fine. But I still wanted it, and I wrongly assumed things would be different if I switched from the Plano to Frisco campus in the fall, which is what I did.

Not a lot changed, only the direction I drove to get to class. My social life was static, but so were my grades, which was a good thing. I tried to dip into the intramural life at Collin, but the team I ended up on made for a rather underwhelming experience in the school's basketball league.

What I really wanted was to go to a four-year university, live on my own and get a taste of the life that had almost passed me by. That would have to wait for now.

***

Despite my dwindling interest in sports journalism, I still wrote for the Legends that fall. It was too good of an opportunity to leave, and the organization was first class in every way.

Jake had finished his time at the University of Texas and was now beginning law school at Southern Methodist University. Brett also graduated college and began graduate school at the University of North Texas. Brian had moved to New York, and T.J. was playing professional basketball overseas after finishing a decorated career at Richmond.

Early in 2017, Jake, Brett and I got to see T.J. play live in Ft. Worth when Richmond played TCU in the NIT. That was an awesome, awesome experience, and my Spider-Man shirt fit perfectly for the Richmond Spiders.

My close friends were all pretty busy that fall, so I had a lot of time on my own at home with not a lot to do – that is, until I figured out what I wanted to do to fill that time.

In *Captain America: The Winter Soldier*, one of the movie's best bits is a journal that Steve Rogers keeps after waking up from nearly 70 years as a "Capsicle," as Tony Stark oh so eloquently put it in *The Avengers*.

The journal is full of things Steve missed and wants to catch up on. The movie cleverly changed up the list for international releases, and the United States' list contains such items like the moon landing, the Berlin Wall (noting that it went up *and* down), *Star Wars* (which is regrettably crossed out for *Star Trek*), and courtesy of his new best friend Sam Wilson, Marvin Gaye's *Troubleman* soundtrack.

Captain America woke up in 2011, at least in the MCU, and I like to think *I* woke up in 2015. It took me almost three years, just like Cap, to make my list, and my list was as follows:

I thought of every single movie, every single song, every single comic book, every single video game, every single thing *of every single thing* that I wanted to watch, listen to, read or play.

I put it all down in a master document that ran dozens of pages long.

It brings a smile to my face to think how long the list got, and I remember that I didn't get to crossing every item off until 2019! And even that statistic is a bit misleading, as the list started up anew again. I had missed so much, and I wanted to catch up on all of it.

I missed my childhood, so now was as good a time as any to live it.

So was born my "Infinity List," a list of my favorite movies that, as of editing this book, just surpassed 700 films. These aren't all the movies I've seen, just the ones with an A+, A or A- rating.

I also created a blog called CGI Fridays, where I wrote about most of the movies I watched – and still do to this day. My writing took a 180-degree turn from the world of sports, and I started to fully commit to entertainment – not as a career path, but as a hobby.

I never really desired to write for a professional publication; I simply enjoyed putting my thoughts down and reading about my own interests. It was therapeutic, it filled the time, and it became my life for the next few years while I toiled the time away in college.

The latter half of 2017 was literally waking up, watching a movie, going to class, coming home and watching another movie, playing video games or reading, *watching a third movie*, then listening to music before bed. I was pulling "three-a-days" and I'm shocked I didn't go mad. Or maybe I did.

When I drove around town, music always came with me. I realize that is not uncommon, but what was unique to my situation was how I listened to music.

Until very recently, I drove a hand-me-down 2005 Ford Explorer named Jarvis that was, ironically, due to his name, technologically challenged. When I began rolling through these music albums and listening to music in the car, I did so by burning CDs. That's me, straight out of a lost decade.

Either way, I was in a good spot as long as I kept myself busy, and in a weird way, all of these recreational things felt productive, like I was doing something good for myself and my well-being.

My treatment, specifically my ERPs, are always the most effective when I'm trying to enjoy myself. So, all of these activities provided the perfect opportunity to test myself – and it was working.

I began to combat my obsessions with anger and frustration, simply wanting to be left alone by them so I could enjoy whichever activity I was on in my rotation. I fought back against the OCD in ways that made me enjoy what I was doing even more and feel a level of accomplishment that only fueled my interest in these activities.

Since I had started seeing Dr. Abel in 2006, I had seen him either three times or twice a month. For the first time, in the later stages of 2017, I was seeing him just once a month.

CHAPTER 24

2018, PART 1 –
CLEANING OUT MY CLOSET

I had taken a lot of big steps in the years leading up to 2018, and I was doing it all from the friendly confines of my parents' Plano home. The itch to move out of the house and live on my own had been festering for a long time.

After all, I was nearly 25 years old and had only left home to go to seven hospitals. That's not exactly what one has in mind when talking about moving out.

In 2017 I had regained my academic footing at Collin College: Plano in the spring, and the Frisco campus in the fall. I was now ready (and eligible) to transfer to a true university and attempt to get back one of the experiences that had passed me by in life.

Everyone talks about how college was the best time of their life – the years they discovered themselves, made long-time friends and lifelong memories. I wanted at least a sip of that.

I had grand aspirations of going somewhere out of state and *really* marking new territory, but my family thought that was a little overzealous, and the safer bet was to stay local. My brother went to the University of Arizona, and I loved that idea, but it wasn't meant to be. Fortunately, there are like nine million colleges to choose from in the DFW metroplex alone.

When I was working for the Rangers the previous summer, I was looking closely at the University of Texas at Arlington. I figured if I held the Rangers job going forward, that would be a convenient place to go to school. As we've learned, that job fell through, and my attention shifted to a school that people in every corner of my life had recommended to me: the University of North Texas.

My dad had a lot of ties to the school, including some property he leases right on campus. He knew the area very well, and it was a chance for me to move out but also stay about 45 minutes from home, which pleased my mother very, very much.

My dad also really wanted me to live in a dorm, if just for a semester. I was resistant, but he was footing the bill, so there was really no debate. His reason was pure: He wanted me to know what it was like to live in a dorm. You know, college stuff.

Some of his most cherished memories are from his time at the University of Texas. The stories he tells about him and his friends at UT play like scenes from *Animal House*. He desperately wanted me to have just a little bit of that, and it was a noble gesture.

I wish I could say it turned out that way, but living in a dorm was a wholly different experience for me. I have to say, though, that I really did enjoy getting out of the house and out from under my parent's umbrella.

I'll be grateful for everything they've done, do and will do for me forever, but it's not an exaggeration to say I've lived a sheltered life. Sure, there were extenuating circumstances, but I basically lived in a protective bubble for a quarter of my life. (Assuming I live to 100, which doesn't seem all that it's cracked up to be.)

My semester living in a dorm revolved around my mysterious roommate. He had a girlfriend and, for the first two months of our life together, he stayed at her place every night. It was a beautiful arrangement. But after spring break, she was at our place every night. She lived in the same dorm, so perhaps her roommate had had enough. I just accepted it, with less than two months to go before I moved out and we parted ways forever.

Overall, he was a good roommate. It could have been a lot worse. I repeat, *a lot worse*. We've all heard the horror stories about bad roommates. The worst thing mine did was spend an unsettling amount of time in the bathroom. I don't think he was doing unspeakable things, I really don't.

Honestly, I think he brought his phone in there whenever he sat on the toilet, which, due to his diet, was multiple times a day, and then he just lost track of time while scrolling through various apps.

That's my best guess, and I'm sticking to it. Every time I knocked, he immediately flushed and got out. So, yeah, that was a thing. Although, sometimes, he didn't get out right away, and I was in a pickle. This was particularly an issue at night when I'd get out of my half-bed, half-workspace contraption, try to open the door for a quick restroom break, and find it locked and unavailable.

I journeyed down to the lobby many nights just to use the bathroom. It was inconvenient, annoying and just weird. But I didn't want to make a thing out of it because of those horror roommate stories. After all I'd been through, I wasn't going to end up on a milk carton.

When we were in the room together, it was pretty much just both of us with our headphones on, watching movies, TV shows or playing video games. And studying, too. How could I forget studying?

I have this habit of humming music while I play games, and my roommate frequently reminded me that I was doing so. But if he had his headphones on, too, how could he hear it? I wasn't that loud. Anyway, horror roommate stories, so I stopped humming.

I got through a lot of long days and nights in my dorm life by revisiting the classic *Batman: Arkham* video game series and playing *MLB The Show*. And who could forget my "Infinity List" of movies, music and comic books? (If you sincerely forgot, I forgive you.)

Perhaps the strangest thing that happened to me while I lived in the dorm was my diet. My dorm was right next to one of the campus cafeterias, and upon entry, I realized it was a vegan cafeteria. I figured I'd try it, and holy no cow, it was delicious! I almost became a full-fledged vegan that semester until my next living space was way on the other side of campus.

Socially, things never materialized at UNT. I admit I can be very stubborn when choosing people I want to get close to or even have a conversation with. I don't like to waste time, and the demographic at UNT was full of people I didn't mesh with.

I don't smoke pot, so that ruled out almost every other person on campus. My hair is brown, not one of the colors of the rainbow, which eliminated me from many social groups. I went to the local gym to play basketball but found it hard to infiltrate any friend groups and make myself a regular.

UNT reminded me of high school in the sense that everyone seemed to already know each other. Friend groups were established, and I was new, as well as much older than many of my classmates. My hobbies and interests did not seem to align with anyone else's, and I had more trouble fitting in anywhere or making friends.

Also, everyone seemed so young. They were quite literally still kids, while I was approaching 25. I've never felt as old as I am, and I certainly don't look it. But I found myself pretty impatient with the immaturity my classmates and housemates possessed.

I joined the school newspaper, the *North Texas Daily*, to try and identify with like-minded people, and also to try and help reignite my love for writing. I went 0 for 2.

In a stroke of good fortune, Brett was at UNT for graduate school and was on campus once a week. We got together before his weekly class to hang out or go see a movie, and that was a big plus to have him around. I looked forward to Wednesdays every week to see him.

I also bumped into an old friend named Chris Blakelely, who I had played club basketball with many years earlier, and we both worked for the Legends in 2016. He was now a basketball assistant at UNT, so I had another point of contact on campus, although I never really saw him due to his busy schedule.

I struggled to build a social life with my classmates. I went to apartment meetings and the UNT rec center, and I tried some extracurricular activities, but nothing seemed to work. I maintain with honesty that it wasn't my pickiness. I was truly a fish out of water at everything I went to.

It didn't help that I've never had much interest in college sports. I think college football games are way too long and taken way too seriously, so there wasn't much interest in getting involved with game days there. I went to the school basketball games because I do like basketball, I could support Chris, and I was always in networking mode, so games were a valuable place to look.

With that said, I had no school spirit. I did not identify with UNT and the Mean Green. I envied the fandom my dad had and still has for his Longhorns, the same as my sister. My mom gets one of her lone pleasures out of life through the Dallas Cowboys. Jake and Brian go crazy for the Mavericks.

I had become numb to sports fandom. Working in the industry definitely did not help. But this made the college experience less impactful for me. I had no school spirit. When the cheerleaders asked the crowd to give them a U, N or T, I simply couldn't do it. I'd be living a lie!

Sometimes I think of myself as a buzzkill. A tad joyless. I suppose all I've been through has given me perspective on what things bring me joy and happiness in life, which are few and far between. So, while I hate to be a downer, I have to admit that few things excite me, and I wasn't getting any excitement out of the college sports scene, which is a natural place to find such passions in this stage of life. UNT isn't really a party school, either, although that's not really my scene anyway.

I just kind of existed in that first semester. I was grateful to be there, to be healthy and to be moving forward in life, and that was good enough.

CHAPTER 25

2018, PART 2 –
WHEN YOU WEREN'T YOUNG

In the summer of 2018, I took four courses, two per summer semester, which was the maximum UNT would allow me to take. It was a lot of work, but I was determined to:

A. Stay busy

B. Be productive, and

C. Graduate as soon as possible.

Even still, I was so incredibly bored for those two to three months. My days were consumed and salvaged by my "Infinity List." I went through so many movies, video games, comic books and albums that summer.

That list literally got into the thousands. It was insane. It became my daily routine to just knock things off it. I was glad to be experiencing things I missed out on over the previous decade, but it became a little nauseating to be doing the same thing every day, albeit with different content.

Still, I discovered some gems, like the original *Planet of the Apes* movies, went back and played the *Star Wars*-inspired *Force Unleashed* video games, dug fully into the musical catalog of *The Killers*, and read the entire *Ultimate Spider-Man* comic book series, all 160 issues, in less than a month.

I watched every Spider-Man animated series, as well as the famous *Batman: The Animated Series* show, and before heading back to Denton, blitzed through my *That '70s Show* DVD collection.

I came to realize that one of the hardest things for me, and this was brought front and center when I went to college, is seeing people happy. Let me explain.

Everyone goes through days of stress, times of anxiety or even bouts of depression. It's different for everyone. Thankfully, we have family and friends and things in life that make it worthwhile, and that's usually what we project externally: happiness.

For me, I project worry. The wrinkles on my forehead and the "look of sadness" people say I have betray me. It's a 24/7 battle that literally enters my dreams. I ritualize and repeat thoughts even while I sleep. It's an odd juxtaposition to the fantasy worlds I also find myself dreaming about.

When I see people living their lives, just going about their business, they seem happy for the most part. Like they are enjoying themselves and living their best life. A college campus is a primary example of that. Classmates laugh and chat together, restaurants are full of groups of people, and the night life is buzzing on UNT's Fry Street and surrounding areas.

I watched all these things from a distance, either walking to or from a night class, or hearing people in my apartment halls or nearby rooms. I would be lying if I said I wasn't jealous of all these people having all these experiences.

It's a time of life I simply missed. When I was 18 and 19 and 20, I was in Boston or Houston or wasting away at home, trying without much effort to make the best of a bad situation.

When I moved from a dorm to an apartment in the fall of 2018, I really, really thought it would change things. I thought my fortunes would turn and I would develop a social circle, find a girlfriend and really start soaking up the college atmosphere.

I was quite excited to move into an apartment, especially as it was a one-bedroom apartment and the only person I would be living with was M-E! The setup was everything I wanted, but my jubilation quickly turned into a serious depression when my hopes and goals didn't come to fruition.

For the first time in a long time, I was completely on my own. It was all that I had wanted for so long, and I was absolutely terrified that it wasn't going according to my optimistic plans. I fell into a deep sadness that I hadn't felt in a few years, and ironically, I ended up going back home to Plano most weekends simply to be around other people.

It got to the point where my dad even asked if I wanted to change schools, but that wasn't practical. He knew that, but he was bummed that I wasn't getting out of college what he did. He had wished that for me, but it started as an unlikely reality that had indeed failed to become one.

I loved the apartment, but those walls were closing in fast when day after day after day became a lonely endeavor. Going home was preferred but also made sense, as I had taken an expanded position with Plano West.

In addition to baseball games in the spring, in 2018 I started announcing their high school football games in the fall, and in the winter, I took over as the voice of their basketball program as well. I've always thought high school football was excessive, especially in Texas where high schools build multi-million-dollar stadiums, but it was a good look on my broadcasting résumé to have the sport everyone took (way too) seriously on there.

Baseball announcing reigns supreme for me, but basketball was a great experience. Channeling my inner "Humble" Billy Hayes and Sean Heath was a blast, and I really looked forward to working the basketball games twice a week. I also did the girls' basketball games in the fall of 2018.

I stayed busy, even taking an 18-hour class load when given the opportunity to advance more quickly through my belated college career. Now officially pursuing broadcast journalism over print journalism, I traded my North Texas newspaper gig for a position at North Texas Television, or NTTV, a student-run television program that had a sports show I became a part of.

Brett was finishing up his graduate degree at UNT, so I still saw him once a week, which was once again a social rescue for me that fall. Other than that, I hung out in my apartment and played video games.

My "Infinity List" of movies was miraculously getting low for the time being, so I dug back into old video game favorites like *The Last of*

Us, Uncharted, Watch Dogs and *Dying Light*, and that September, *Marvel's Spider-Man* was released and met every possible expectation.

Video games, along with movies, were my go-to ways to pass the time. And I had a lot of time to pass. I understand completely why people say, "Life is short," but days can be long! I've never been a great sleeper either, so filling time at night has always been a chore.

With a lot of time came a very determined focus on my *MLB The Show* Miami Marlins franchise, and I went to the World Series in the game for the first time in as long as I could remember. I blew a late Game 6 lead and then lost to the Houston Astros in Game 7, but it was fun while it lasted. I guess I couldn't escape my Texas Rangers blood.

The other way to fill time would be writing, and I continued to put everything I had into my work with the Legends, who graciously kept me on board while I wrote from a distance. When I went into Plano, I ventured to Frisco whenever I could to work a game in person and see the staff, but I mostly wrote and did my work remotely.

I was no longer doing any other sports writing except my required duties with the Legends, but I am happy to report that I did finally rediscover my passion for writing. It actually happened in the classroom, but not in the way my professors would like to think.

In college, classes are sometimes hours long. In the UNT journalism program, there are several classes that run three hours at a time. They are usually once a week, but that's a long time to sit in one place and hear lectures that have absolutely no appeal.

Laptops in classrooms are a given nowadays, so I began to write during class. Professor Loftis and Bagley, if you're reading this, yes, I still took notes, but I had multiple tabs open.

To pass the time, and perhaps keep my sanity, I wrote in class and began to write even more at home. I opened my CGI Fridays blog back up and started to fill it with a ton of new content. I even expanded to music and video games and, for the first time in a couple years, I started to love writing again. I looked forward to my next opportunity to add to my blog, and the entries are extensive to this day.

I love to organize things, perhaps too much, just like I was so meticulous about my morning itinerary, even as an adolescent. In that same spirit, I enjoy ranking things, and I did a whole lot of that to bide my time during class and during many lonely nights.

I ranked movies by year and by various categories. I ranked my favorite video games and musicians. I even ranked film composers. I really experienced a passion for this writing, something I hadn't felt in a while, and, ironically, it was the first writing in years that I was doing for free.

It was for one purpose, really. It was for me.

My means of passing the time during these lonely days was to first build my class schedule as intermittently as possible. If I could space them out during the day and over the course of the week, I did so. I was *that guy* who didn't mind having a single Friday class, as long as it meant having something to do that day.

At night during these times, the plan was always to keep myself occupied by scratching items off the "Infinity List." I watched movies, played video games and read comic books until nighttime, and then I could flip a sports game on until it was time for bed.

Doing things I liked also meant naturally performing ERPs, as they are most effective when I'm simply trying to do something I want to do. They are least effective when I'm down in the dumps because I'm already feeling bad. Ironically, when I'm depressed, it's easier to fight off intrusive thoughts. I'm less motivated to deal with them in my low moments, as I'm already feeling crappy.

But when I'm in a good mood and enjoying myself, or when things are going well in my life, my thoughts become incredibly difficult to manage. I always like to say, "OCD doesn't want you to be happy." It attacks strongest when you're in a good place – a rarity for me. So, if there was some twisted consolation to being depressed, it made my OCD symptoms seem like an afterthought to plain old depression.

Shortly before I went to college, my evening habits began to change. I would flip a baseball or basketball game on, but I realized I was no longer actually watching. My laptop was always open during games, and I would write, read or do both concurrently while a game played in the background.

As a kid, I watched my local teams intently and intensely. Full focus. Now, I had a nationally broadcasted game on, as I had grown to loathe local television crews. I wasn't as invested, and my deteriorating interest in sports has been well documented by now.

But having a game on at night was simply what I had always done. It felt weird *not* to have a game on and *not* end my day this way. It felt more like an obligation, or a ritual, to watch a game at night – and to keep a foot in the sports world's door, as it was my college major and current career choice.

Soon, nights belonged to the same things that occupied my days: movies, gaming and reading. I've always been a man of simple tastes, like the Joker, although our habits are, thankfully, pretty different.

Every day began to run together for me. Wake up, start a movie, go to class, go back to my apartment, finish the movie, go to another class, come back, play video games, read, start another movie, go to another class and then finish that second movie until I fell asleep.

Mixed in there would be Legends games that I watched on my laptop so I could write my postgame articles. I would also drive back into Plano once or twice a week to announce a football, basketball or baseball game, whatever was in season.

Many of those games came on Fridays, as is typical in a high school sports schedule, so I would just stay the night in Plano that night as well as Saturday.

I joined a local softball league in Plano/Frisco, and it became a routine to just stay back at home over the weekend, play my softball game and then drive back to Denton that afternoon.

It wasn't the college life I wanted, but things were still moving in the right direction. My hopes and dreams to expand my social life and form a dating life hadn't come to fruition, but I had my health.

Until it almost slipped away.

CHAPTER 26

2019 – THE REBOOT

As 2018 came to a close, I suffered my first legitimate relapse in a long, long time. My OCD had been in check – it wasn't perfect because that's impossible – but I had held it steady for a few years now.

OCD, like life, according to Jeff Goldblum in *Jurassic Park*, "Uh, finds a way." Mental illness is like a virus. You can fight it and treat it, but you can't cure it. My obsessive thoughts mutated and matured, just as I had in my emerging life. All the tricks of the trade, all the ERP treatments and mental traps I had created to manage my mental state – they all began to falter.

I started to believe that my years of work, my hard-earned progress, was going to fall apart. These kinds of scares happened rather frequently, as I was and am always vulnerable to my brain's whims, but it hadn't felt this real, this scary, in a long time.

Though I was meeting with Dr. Abel just once a month now, and sometimes even over the phone because I was at school, he never hesitated to remind me at the end of our sessions that he was always available if I needed him.

Thankfully, I hadn't needed his immediate help in a while. But on a particularly low December day in 2018, right after that semester of school had concluded, I needed him.

I tried to put off the call, knowing that it validated my setback, but after multiple rounds of frustrated tears, it was time to pick up the phone.

As usual when it comes to all things Dr. Abel, it was the right move. We talked for an hour or so, his calm, reassuring voice exactly what I needed in that moment. He asked if I was continuing to do my ERPs, how my depression and anxiety were, and how I was generally dealing with my current life's situation.

Something I said piqued his interest. I mentioned how unhappy I was, but the reason was that I felt lost. I had just about fully lost my drive for the sports journalism and broadcasting industry, despite a considerable breakthrough at UNT.

That winter, I joined play-by-play man John Liddle as the voice of the UNT Women's Basketball team. John was a fill-in broadcaster for the Legends, and I learned of his role with the Mean Green, a happy coincidence.

Upon reaching out, he was gracious enough to offer me the role as his color commentator on the official radio station of the UNT basketball program. It was a sizable leap from student-run productions and a huge opportunity for me and my career.

Except even this couldn't reignite my passion for what I was going to school for. I had lost interest and faith in my major.

I relayed to Dr. Abel how this made me feel, and he asked the question I had refused to ask myself for some time now.

"Why?"

Why pursue a career you don't want? I felt truly destined to work in the sports industry, and figured I would eventually settle into it, even if I didn't feel the same way about sports as I did as a kid.

He asked me what I wanted to do, and I wasn't sure.

When I first went to college, my minor was education. Because of time and an estimated graduation date, I switched to psychology to expedite my college timeline. But there was a reason I chose education in the first place.

Deep down in me, there was a passion for teaching that I never really explored. I've always been great with kids, claiming that my true "superpower" is the power of patience, a trait that makes a world of difference with people of all ages, but especially youngsters.

Part of me feels like I was meant to be a teacher. Two of my mom's siblings, my Uncle David and Aunt Robin, were both teachers.

Countless students were extremely lucky to have them in their lives, just as I was. The impact they made was the one I wanted to make on others.

I had buried this career path away but was now looking at it in a new light – a light that subsequently had gone off in my head.

This epiphany set me on a new course. It didn't solve my resurgent OCD thoughts, but it alleviated my anxiety and, therefore, calmed my depression. I look back on that phone call with Dr. Abel as a crucial moment in my life, as so many moments with him have been.

He advised me not to give up on my broadcasting career and cautioned me against making an overnight decision. It was important to not only keep working hard with the Legends and with the UNT basketball team, but it was just as important to simply keep working.

Who knew what conclusion I would eventually come to? I am admittedly a fickle person, always looking for the "next thing" in life, never feeling satisfied.

Still, when I talked things out with the good doctor, and put every variable on the table, I was able to see that what was really troubling me was an internal identity struggle, not another relapse.

***

As time went by, so did my junior year of college. I nursed my OCD symptoms throughout the beginning half of 2019, eagerly awaiting *Avengers: Endgame* in April, but I was also careful of my thoughts that always flare up when I'm looking forward to something.

To prepare for the end of Marvel's "Infinity" saga, the historical culmination of 22 films dating back to 2008, I mapped out an MCU marathon schedule with Jake. We got together mostly every weekend starting early in 2019, and we literally finished *Avengers: Infinity War* the week before *Endgame* premiered.

During that same time, I also marathon-ed *Star Wars* with Brett, who, despite sharing similar film interests, had never seen the OG franchise all the way through. I took him through the prequels, *Rogue One*, the original trilogy, and then cut things off at *Episode VII* before the films turned to the dark side with number eight.

These dueling marathons kept my mind focused on something during the spring semester of my junior year, and it was a wonderful privilege to be able to get together with Jake and Brett almost every weekend to watch movies.

This all led to Avengers opening night, which I attended with Jake and Brett, a Marvel tradition we had begun in 2017.

Highlights of that spring definitely include the time with my friends, but I also had an incredible time and an even more incredible learning experience calling the UNT Women's Basketball games with John Liddle.

From my first game at the storied Moody Coliseum at SMU, to the Conference USA Women's Basketball Tournament that finished during spring break in March, that experience goes down as one of the best in my sports broadcasting career.

Working with someone like John, a mentor of mine amongst several in the industry, taught me a lot. As summer began, I went to breakfast with another friend and mentor, Mark Followill.

I expressed to him in total honesty the doubts I had been having about my career path. Between delicious bites at The Original Pancake House, he said something to me that really hit home.

"To work in this industry, you have to be a fan."

It seems so simple. To work in sports, you need to love sports. And for a long time, I honestly hadn't loved the game. Sure, I liked it. I liked it a lot. But he said that wasn't enough – you have to be passionate to dedicate your career to it.

That summer, to fulfill an internship credit for my journalism degree, I undertook an internship at a familiar place. I reached back out to the RoughRiders, and for about three weeks that summer, I shadowed the team's radio play-by-play voice, Ryan Rouillard, and created my own mock broadcasts from the game I was watching.

I also got to spend some time behind the public address microphone with Sean Heath, the Mavericks regular who also did some summertime work with the RoughRiders.

It was during these broadcasts and this internship, experiences someone legitimately working toward a job in the industry would relish, that I finally called it.

I fully realized while doing these broadcasts that I just wasn't into it anymore. And that was a deciding moment. With all the guidance I had received, and all the back-and-forth I'd gone through the past couple years, and particularly the last few months, I decided early in the summer of 2019 that I was officially switching careers.

***

My parents were surprised. They knew about my doubts, but they figured, like everyone else, that this lifelong sports fanatic would eventually come back around and fulfill his destiny in the industry he was meant to work in. I thought it would happen, too.

Part of me hoped it would. Part of me hoped it *wouldn't*. And it didn't. The next step was figuring out what I wanted to do next, and there were really only a couple of options I was considering.

For a moment, I considered what kind of career I could make out of my love and knowledge of movies, which had become my number one hobby over the last several years.

I threw around the idea of becoming a movie critic, but there's really no such thing anymore. Maybe an author, writing science fiction novels, but that idea didn't stick. Especially after my sports experience, I didn't really want to work in the film industry and sour that fantasy world, too.

I quickly circled back to the idea that had been lying beneath the surface all along: teaching.

Just like I had done in my "old" life, I quickly worked on building connections in the teaching industry. This happened rather quickly, with a family friend working nearby as an administrator in Allen, Texas. Her mother had also been a teacher and administrator, so they were stockpiled with tips.

I asked for advice on how, where and when to get started. Since I was no longer minoring in education, I would have to get an alternate certification license to teach. This meant enrolling in what is called an "alt-cert" program, and I set my sights on that ASAP.

***

Saying goodbye to the sports industry was bittersweet, as it had been my quarter-lifelong dream. I had been working a writing and/or broadcasting gig since I was in middle school, so closing this chapter of my life was a big step. But it was a big step *forward*.

Leaving the Legends was difficult. That opportunity was so big and so important. Moreso, that experience was nothing but a great time. It was also a positive, family-like environment, something you seldom experience in the adult world. I continued to write some articles for them here and there, but they were aware that I would not be returning for the 2020 season.

Despite leaving that line of work, I continued to announce games for the Plano West baseball team. Speaking of family, that felt like it, too. Plus, despite no longer doing traditional journalism, I still very much enjoyed public address announcing and could absolutely see myself doing that in the future.

Soon, I was signed up in the Region 10 certification program, and another new chapter of life was beginning. It was a lot of work, and a lot of time, and hitting the restart button meant it would be a long road, but it was all worth it.

It took a lot of time, and a whole lot of change happened very fast, but I was used to that in my life. I would do whatever it took to do something that my heart was set on.

At last, I had found what I wanted. What I needed.

Purpose.

CHAPTER 27

2020 – THE BEGINNING

2020 was an odd year.

On a personal level, 2020 did indeed mark my beginning. Or at least a new beginning. I'll never forget all that I went through to get to this point, but this year put "real life" in my life's equation. I had a sense of normalcy, something I did not know very well at all.

As 2019 departed, I was making great strides and looking optimistically to my new, revised future as a teacher. Becoming a teacher is, ironically, an expensive process. Not ironically, it's also extensive, as becoming an educator and caretaker of the future members of society ought to be.

In October 2019, I took and passed the first of a series of state exams required to become a teacher. I'd take the next one in the summer of 2020, and I finished the brunt of work for my certification program by the end of the summer.

My last semester of college was nothing out of the ordinary, until everything was out of the ordinary. In March 2020, the whole world got turned upside down in the form of a global pandemic.

I actually completed my student teaching hours the first week of March, just before everything went virtual. My teaching internship took place minutes from my childhood home at Renner Middle school, where I went to school in sixth and seventh grade before transitioning to private school.

Returning to Renner was like a dream – or a nightmare. That's where I was when everything went sideways in 2006. School, after my house, was the place I struggled the most. That makes logical sense, as it was the only place other than my home where I spent any substantial amount of time.

Not a lot had changed in 14 years. The hallways were full of kids, eyes wide with wonder and their whole lives ahead of them.

Some of the same teachers still taught there. New teachers showed me around, and we reminisced about how things were different, yet all the same.

After the government shutdown, my college career ended on Zoom without much fanfare. I was only taking two courses for a total of six hours in the spring, so honestly, I already felt done.

It all felt very anticlimactic, but that's a rather apt description for the college experience I ended up having.

Not until weeks after I officially graduated (although I didn't attend my graduation, just as I hadn't in high school), did it sink in that I had accomplished the goal I once thought was unachievable. A goal three and a half long – yet also remarkably quick – years in the making.

The moment that brought it home was when my diploma arrived in the mail, and my mom showed it to me. There are moments in life when you know your parents are proud. Not like after-a-tee-ball game proud, or getting-an-A-on-a-hard-test proud, but like *proud* proud.

Nobody had been in my corner more than my mom. Along with my dad, nobody had gone through the pain, suffering and turmoil that accompanied those 15 trying years more than her.

Nobody sought to understand this thing called OCD more than my mom, desperately trying to make sense of this unexplainable disease. And nobody believed more that I could go back to college and finish a goal that seemed so improbable for so long.

So, when she showed me the diploma, tears in her eyes, I couldn't help but cry, too. It was a proud moment, and one I'll hold close until my time is up in this crazy world.

***

The spring and summer of 2020 became a test of filling time. Just like the rest of the world, I couldn't go anywhere, do anything or see anyone. Luckily for me, I had plenty of practice in this arena.

I used these quarantine days to work on my teaching certificate and apply for jobs, and I started a project I had talked about doing for years, but never found the right frame of mind to actually begin: this book.

I crafted an outline for the book at the UNT Starbucks in the fall of 2018, but I pushed the idea aside until I could really focus on it: after school ended and before work began. That way I could give this story the attention it deserved.

Writing this book was also an intense form of ERP. Reliving all these moments, most of them buried deep in my mind, would be an emotional rollercoaster. Putting it all on paper was a daunting task.

***

My career choice of teaching came with an added bonus: I would also be coaching. At first, I was aiming to teach elementary school, but once I decided I should also put my sports knowledge and experience to use, I shifted to middle school so I could do more than lead PE, but coach actual, specific sports.

When things started opening back up in June, I called an old friend from my early days at Plano West. His dad used to coach at the high school and now coached a summer team, which in turn was rostered by several kids I knew, and I also knew their fathers very well.

I caught on with that group and helped coach that team during June and July. The experience was everything I could have hoped for, save for extremely long drives all over Texas to reach fields that weren't closed due to the pandemic.

The part I enjoyed most wasn't the baseball but being around the kids. I enjoy being around young people – as I've said, I tend to live vicariously through them, experiencing second-hand the childhood I never had.

I continued to apply for open teaching and coaching positions, which in Texas are grouped into one application at the middle and high school levels. Time went by, and no offers came in, so I looked into the possibility of being a substitute teacher for the 2020-2021 school year.

I've harped on the importance of business connections multiple times, but nobody does the connections game better than my mom. Part of that is because she is a doctor and sees a thousand patients per day, which somehow is only *slightly* an exaggeration. She is well respected, well connected and beloved by all.

In mid-July, she started doing a little digging on my behalf, and within a week, I had a Zoom interview with a middle school in Frisco, Texas. The next day, I got my first big-boy job.

July 27, 2020, marked my first day. What happened in the next year was proof that I made the right choice.

I searched for so long and in so many places for my true purpose. To do something that, in my heart, I truly believed mattered. That made a difference.

I thought it was one thing for many, many years. But after a year of working with kids and doing everything in my power to make a positive impact on their lives and, therefore, the world, I have found my purpose.

I'm happy, I'm healthy, I'm making a difference, I'm living my life and I'm so OCD.

EPILOGUE: "MR. BRIGHTSIDE"

One of the greatest songs ever written is "Mr. Brightside" by The Killers. Penned by lead singer Brandon Flowers, the song begins with a lyric that I really identify with – be sure to look it up if you don't already know it. Use Google, not Bing.

My primary goal in writing *I'm So OCD* is to bring awareness to the unheard, underrepresented community that suffers every single moment of every single day from obsessive compulsive disorder.

It can be a lonely life. A miserable life. Not even a life at all. And for many, that's the way it remains. I'm so lucky to come from a family with the means to address my mental health needs. It's not cheap. And it's hard to find help – even harder to find *good* help.

Sure, I want to tell my story. But I really want to tell my *success* story. I want people in this world that suffer from any mental illness to know that there is a light at the end of the tunnel. It may be a 15-year long tunnel, and a tunnel that truly never ends, but *there is* light.

There is hope.

I spent years refusing to believe I would find it. Instead, I thought I would never escape my demons, and the best life I could live would be a marginalized existence. It took a lot of help, a lot of time and a lot of unwavering support from my family and my doctors to make it back. To get back to the real world and do something with my life.

In *The Dark Knight*, Harvey Dent says, "The night is darkest just before the dawn."

This quote acknowledges that bad things are going to happen, but it also reminds us that good things are coming. Of course, Dent ends up turning into the villain Two-Face, but I'm happy to report that did not happen to me.

I constantly reflect about the life I've lived. And the life I'm living. And the life I've yet to live. There's hopefully a lot more of it left.

I have a lot of regrets, none bigger than missing my childhood. But for as bad as things *were*, I can feel pretty good about them now.

***

No day goes by where OCD isn't a threat. There is no cure. It's always there and it always will be unless a miraculous medical breakthrough happens in my lifetime.

My every waking moment is full of constant brain activity, most of it unwanted obsessive thoughts. But over the years, I've become a pro at handling them. That doesn't mean I'm immune. I still get "stuck," and I still do ERPs multiple times a day.

I do them at home, I do them at work. I do them in my dreams and wake up wondering how that's even possible.

I still have crippling anxiety that requires my constant attention. I get depressed often, mostly when I think about all that I have missed. Time I'll never get back. Memories that will never be made. Part of my existence that will never be.

But to stress over these things is to dwell on something I can't control. Not long ago, I made a commitment to myself to be hopeful. Promising eternal happiness isn't a reasonable goal, but something *I can* be is eternally *hopeful*.

I am dedicated to making a positive impact on this world, and I have found my way to do so. I am dedicated to seeing the best in people, no matter what. I am dedicated to making every day count, from the little things like having "me time," to big things like teaching and coaching the next generation.

My future is in my hands, and I intend to make the most of it. For myself, and for others.

I've come out of my cage, and I'm doing just fine. I'm "Mr. Brightside."
Asher Feltman will return.

ANECDOTES

ARLENE JACOBS, MOTHER

Asher,

I'm not sure how to begin. Do I start with the sadness I felt as a physician and mother that I couldn't initially help you, my son? Or the desperation I felt as a parent due to my inadequacies in helping to free you from the disease trapped in your brain? Or do I start with the celebration of your remarkable and unusual success to beat those devils? All are so very important, and you have documented this incredible journey for yourself, your family and for the many undiagnosed and diagnosed OCD sufferers and their families and friends too.

I recall the night when I tried so hard to get you to sleep after your rituals and get you to bed. You asked, at age 12, "If you are a surgeon, Mom, can't you just cut these bad thoughts out of my brain? You cut things out of your patients and cure them." Just one of the numerous wishes and answers I couldn't provide you.

I, unfortunately, recall a lot of awful nights for Dad and I watching you suffer, panic, even try to end your life, just to rid yourself of the awful wiring of your brain. I remember the pills, more pills, therapies, the isolation, all because your diagnosis did not have a logical explanation. It's something that many today still do not understand.

We went to numerous hospitals and doctors, and spent horrific days and especially nights to finally get to a diagnosis and understanding of this disease. We finally landed the incredible expertise of Dr. Robinson and Dr. Abel. Your persistence to "beat this," and the undying love of your family, along with the fortunate blessing that we have the means to get you all you could possibly need, got us there.

No stone unturned. I know these stones persist, but I know now, as do you, your strengths, your weaknesses, your desire to teach and educate those in need, and your ability to ignore on a daily basis these intrusive thoughts. You will continue to grow and provide knowledge and hope to those that suffer also.

Lessons learned, for sure. And your message from the beginning that OCD is not a trait (I still cringe when people use this as an adjective), but an awful disease that, while not curable, is livable. I will always be so proud of you, Asher. You deserve so much. Keep on educating the world.

ALLEN FELTMAN, FATHER

Asher, I always wanted you to have a great life, and watching you suffer those years just killed your mom and me. I wish I had more patience during the trying times, but it sapped the heart out of me daily. Writing this book made me aware of the depth and seems like therapy for you. Your path looks promising!

ALEC FELTMAN, BROTHER

I want to start this by saying that I am truly upset with myself for
how I treated my younger brother during a time in his life when he
needed me most. I am embarrassed by what I have said, the anger
I showed and the ignorance I displayed during those years in
which he battled this terrible disease. I always think back to those
times when I acted in those negative ways toward my amazing
brother – and I feel disgusted that I treated him so poorly.

From an older brother's perspective – one who loves his
younger brother so much – I wished repeatedly for him to be at
peace. Peace within the mind while awake and active – and peace
while asleep. It was very tough to watch him struggle with daily
tasks that I thought were easy. Little did I know what he was going
through mentally to do such things as open the door, go up the
stairs or brush his teeth.

I know he had frustrations with me as well during his struggle.
Knowing Asher, he would look at me during those times and beg
for me to understand. There were many moments he vocalized
his frustration with me, and even more moments where his eyes
showed his internal frustration. But being my stubborn self, I was
too wrapped up in my own issues to even notice. Shame on me.

Asher and I have so many things in common, and he is my mini-
me in so many ways. Looking at pictures of us as children, it was
hard to tell the difference between the two of us. Asher does have
a kinder smile and a gentler soul, so determining who was who
was easier once those features started to really show around the
time he was eight years old.

There are many stories of how I acted toward Asher during this
time of his life, but I felt that I was doing what was best for him. I
wanted him to grow up and become the man I knew he could be.
I pushed and pushed for him to become more like me, but little
did I know that he was already a better version. It didn't take me

acting how I did for him to become the person we see here today. If anything, I may have made it worse, but Asher can overcome anything, and he sure overcame my negative actions.

I love this guy and I hate that he had to go through something so terrible for so many years, but I am so proud to call him my brother and he is the strongest person I have – and will ever – meet.

ADRIENNE CHERNOFF, SISTER

I don't think I'll ever cry more tears than the ones I've cried over my brother. I thought I lost my smiling, obnoxiously intelligent, know-it-all, hardheaded Asher forever. The change in his personality seemed to happen so slowly in the moment, but when I think back, he so quickly became a ghost of himself. Although he lived right across the hall from me, and we'd continue to have meals and conversations together, it was as if he was never fully there. Little did I know that my younger brother was being tortured inside, and as his big sister, I became angry when he made excuses not to be around us, rather than understanding of the thoughts burdening his day-to-day life. I blamed myself for not being able to help him overcome his negative thoughts by trying to force happy moments onto him. Why couldn't he just push these negative thoughts away? Why could I not be the heroic big sister that would help make him better? Why couldn't he just be my Ash again?

Time stood still in my world involving Asher. While I was graduating high school, then college and becoming more of a young adult, Asher's life remained stagnant. At first, I was furious that I would never have the brother-sister bond I thought I selfishly deserved: the kind my aunt and dad had as best friend-siblings, who truly enjoyed life together as friends and not because they were related. Just like the stages of grief, this anger passed, and

I accepted that Asher and I would never have the bond I dreamed of. Instead, our relationship would be one of disabled brother and caretaker. I made a promise to myself that when the time came, Asher would live with me for the remainder of his life. I was even prepared to tell my future husband that this was non-negotiable.

There isn't an exact moment when I realized Asher was becoming my Asher again, but I no longer feel the need to be his caretaker, and I can just be his protective big sister.

We have come a long way in understanding OCD in our family – it's not something that just goes away. I used to feel that OCD was all that would define Asher, but now it is just one of the obstacles he has to deal with daily. Asher is still annoyingly smart and hardheaded, but this disease has also gifted him with patience, empathy and a greater understanding of those around him. I hate the memories and experiences OCD took away from Asher and our family but I'm optimistic that the worst is behind us.

Today, I continue to cry more tears for Asher because I've never been prouder of anyone in my life.

FRED RABINOWITZ, UNCLE

My regret is that I didn't know what I didn't know. When you were a young child, I thought it was so cute that you had to have all your elephants lined up in just the right order. You had to wear the "right" shirt. When playing a game, we had to make a move or play a card in just the right order. Now, looking back, these were all signs of what was to come. Perhaps if we recognized this as OCD behavior, we could have addressed it sooner. If you sharing your journey helps one parent, uncle or loved one to recognize the signs, then you have made a huge impact.

DEBBIE RABINOWITZ, AUNT

There were so many times that Asher seemed lost in his own world. Our families are extremely close, and I have always considered him one of my own.

As a young boy, Asher showed signs of frustration. His toys would have to be in the correct line or order, he would quit or mess up a game in anger if he was not winning. He was annoyed if things were not going his way.

This progressed to behavior of being "stuck" in a car or shower and not being able to function predictably in his daily life. He then seemed to develop "demons" in his thoughts. Notably, anyone with some type of visual deformity, someone overweight or a smoker would set him off into a state of mind that no one could really understand.

One evening at a pizza restaurant, a young boy was sitting across the room from us. He was overweight and may have looked a little funny. Asher saw him and delved into a trance of fear. Asher perceived this child as some horrible creature and looked as if he actually feared for his own life. Whatever the thoughts were, they were real to Asher. They caused a display of uncontrollable vocal and mechanical tics, and a look in Asher's eyes that I will never forget. I looked at Asher, and then at the other boy. I saw an innocent boy eating pizza with his family, and I wondered so much what Asher was seeing.

After countless hours of struggling, therapy, family support, special schools and psychiatric facilities, Asher has fought to become an amazing young man.

He is one of the smartest, kindest, most caring and honest young men you could imagine. I know that he still struggles with some things, but he has found a way to keep himself on the right path. He has found a way to "give back" to neutralize a horrific childhood, and perhaps help someone else. He has found the love of teaching.

Asher's journey has been something that is very difficult to perceive, understand or explain. All I know is that he made it through with flying colors!

I love this boy with all my heart and know that he will be okay!

HARRIS RABINOWITZ, COUSIN

Truly, I didn't understand at the time. I think it was the time around your Bar Mitzvah. The Mavs were in the championship or something like that. I remember seeing the disease. I remember specifically a couple times when we used to lower the rim in your driveway and play basketball. I remember you having a few outbursts or whatever you want to call it. Anger was something I saw out of you, but looking at it now, it was probably internal frustration. I remember being confused. I remember being cautious. But what I remember most was the pain I saw on your face.

You know that feeling when you can see someone thinking? Well, I had that feeling, but it was pain and suffering. I can't remember the exact day, but I know I was there, I know you were there, and I know this was the day I knew something wasn't right. I've always had love in my heart for my family. I recognized the pain and anguish right away, and this was just the beginning. I remember feeling like I needed to be careful in what I did or said around you.

At school, I remember hearing people talk about it, saying things like, "Dude, what's wrong with Asher?" I remember saying, "Nothing is wrong," but I knew something was. I didn't fully understand myself, so how could they understand?

In my opinion, we all go through something. I just want to say how proud I am of you. You battled the entire way and are still fighting every day. That says a lot about you, Ash. You're a warrior in more ways than most people. It's something I think about often. It motivates me when I think I'm having a "bad day" or whatever. I think about all the people in my life who truly set examples. Amongst the very few people who I look up to, it's a short list. And when I'm down or lazy or whatever it is, I think about the battle that all these people have been through, and it drives me. You drive me. Ash, you're my best friend.

It was interesting to witness. Someone I knew so well had become a totally different human in a matter of weeks. It for sure caused a little ripple in our relationship as well. But not for a moment did I stop loving you. I think there was a time when our "friendship" didn't develop as I wish it would have, but I feel we've made up for that in the more recent years. Thirteen-year-olds didn't understand. I didn't understand.

But I will say something I did recognize right off the bat was progress/change. There were a couple of really bad years, but I recognized immediately when things started to progress. You went through war, and you succeeded. You should be extremely proud of yourself. I'm proud for you.

I remember people making comments or insults like, "Your cousin is crazy," or "Your cousin has a wild temper," or whatever it was. My instinct was always to protect my family and my friends. You are both. But I also saw some of those things they saw. I remember the challenges of navigating high school. I remember feeling protective. I'm not sure if I did a good enough job on that. And not that you necessarily needed protection, but I remember it was a big deal at school. I remember being sensitive to it. I remember it as if they were talking about me. Everyone would ask me about it like I knew what was going on. I didn't know anything.

I remember some of the hardships you had internally with your father and your brother and sister. I remember you coming over to

my parents' almost to "get away." I actually give Miley about 2.2%
of credit for the victory you had over OCD!

It's just so weird how life unfolds. People either sink or swim
when they are faced with challenges. You are a swimmer. Moreso,
you are a winner.

I remember our whole family always talking about your illness
and what we could do about it. My dumbass always kind of
thought it would work itself out naturally – big life lesson for me.
Nothing works itself out. You have to battle and work for what you
want. You did this. You did it.

Ash, you're a gem. You're smart, you're comical, you're good
looking (since you look somewhat like me!), and your confidence
in yourself increases every time I see you. I'm very proud of you,
but also you are someone who I look up to.

I really don't care what you do with this (anecdote). Mix it,
mash it, throw it in the trash. I don't care. I just want you to know
what an impact you made on me, and I'm sure other people.
You're a warrior. You can do anything, and the people in this world
who are friends with you pick that up from you and your story.

In my opinion, your OCD doesn't define you. What defines you
is the love you have for your family, the love you have for your
friends and the ability to f*cking battle for what you need.

Love you dude. I won't ever forget playing Ken Griffey (Baseball
on Nintendo 64), or baseball in the den upstairs. Once you make
millions on the book, Casey, our kiddos and I are moving in.

ADAM CHERNOFF, BROTHER-IN-LAW

I met Asher in early 2019, shortly after his sister and I started
dating. He was finishing his undergrad degree and in the process

of changing majors from sports broadcasting/journalism to teaching. I remember brief discussions with his sister, mom and dad explaining the reason why he was still in school as a 27-year-old. They informed me of his previous struggles, something I would never have known based on our interactions. Plus, everyone has their own journey.

We became closer in June 2019 after a family vacation, and we bonded over our strong affection for movies of almost all genres. This is where I saw the first sign of OCD, when he explained his movie ranking list and could recite where movies were on said list. I didn't really think much of it, chalking it up to a passion, but with each new movie coming out, the list would change and evolve. The next sign I saw was when we traveled. The entire family would check a bag, except Asher. He wanted to make sure he always had it with him.

I would never have known how sick Asher was as a youth unless being told otherwise. Now in 2022, Asher is not only my brother-in-law (guess things worked out with his sister!), but also a good friend.

JAKE WINSLETT, BEST FRIEND

I remember feeling confused and shocked when Asher was first diagnosed. We had just started sixth grade, the first year of middle school. Asher and I had grown incredibly close by the end of elementary school, primarily bonding over our mutual adoration of Dallas sports teams. We had also just established Asher's new-found love of *Star Wars* (*Episode III - Revenge of the Sith* had just come out the previous summer, which was Asher's introduction to *Star Wars*). At this point in our young lives, it was rare for us to go more than a few days without seeing each other. It goes without saying, then, that Asher's diagnosis and subsequent move to Houston was upsetting to me. One day, we were dunking on each other on the lowered basketball hoop in Asher's driveway. The next day, he was gone.

I remember a rush of emotions going through my mind, most of which were selfishly centered around the fact that Asher was going away. At first, I thought that there must have been some sort of misunderstanding, because in the seemingly endless amount of time we had spent together I never would have thought that anything was "wrong." Then, I remember a subtle feeling of guilt. After all, he was one of my best friends. How wouldn't I have noticed if something was going on? Was there nothing I could have done to help?

After the initial shock of Asher's diagnosis and departure waned, my thoughts shifted to trying to understand his condition. Because we were just middle schoolers, it was hard for me to comprehend what Asher was going through. At that time, I knew other kids our age who had been diagnosed with ADD/ADHD – but Asher's diagnosis was the first time I had heard about OCD. I remember asking adults what OCD was and what it meant for Asher, and I quickly realized that the average person knew very little about OCD. Most of the answers I got were something along the lines of, "It's a condition that impacts people in different ways." It frustrated me to feel so in the dark about something one of my best friends was experiencing.

While Asher has taught me a lot about OCD and his experience with it over the last 15-plus years, I recognize that, in a lot of ways, I'm still in the dark with respect to the full extent of the impact it's had on him. I'm incredibly proud of Asher for opening himself up and sharing his experience with OCD in this book. I have no doubt that it will help others who have been diagnosed with OCD. But perhaps just as importantly, it will help those like myself who can't possibly appreciate the day-to-day of living with OCD.

CREDITS

The list of people to thank starts and ends with my parents. They sacrificed so much, not to mention a sizable portion of their earnings, to get me the help I needed. It took years for the hard work to pay off, but we did it. And I quite literally could not have done it – or done anything at all – without you. Thanks for having kid number three.

My siblings had the tall task of growing up with me. On most days, nobody understood what was happening to me. On our best days, we managed to have dinner together without incident. It was an unusual upbringing, with my brother's diabetes, my OCD and my sister's ability to navigate it all like the future doctor she has become.

The Rabinowitzes have been more than an aunt, uncle and cousins. They are my second family in so many ways. Their door was always open. Literally. They used to forget to lock it all the time.

All my life, I've also had the privilege of a second mom. That person is Carmen Flores. She's as much family as Mom, Dad, Alec or Adrienne. Thank you, Carmenita.

I went through many doctors until I found two that helped. Helped is an understatement, and more than 15 years later, I still see both Dr. Abel and Dr. Robinson. Their expertise, guidance and professional abilities as psychologists and psychiatrists, respectively, changed my life and gave me a chance to be more than my sickness.

Thank you, Dirk Nowitzki. Not just a great athlete, but a great man. A true role model for a kid who desperately needed a hero.

Thank you, George Lucas. The creator of a universe, against all odds, whose imagination alone changed the lives of so many for the better – mine included.

Thank you, Stan Lee. Much like *Star Wars*, nobody thought Spider-Man was a good idea. He followed his heart and created the character anyway, changing the world forever. In his own words, "Maybe what I'm doing isn't really unimportant. Maybe entertainment is one of the most important things."

Thank you, Chris Evans. You showed me that fictional superheroes can be real superheroes. You aren't just Captain America, you're a force for good in the real world.

Thank you, Frank Catalanotto, whose versatility as a player, leadership as a man and funky batting stance helped me learn to hit left-handed. Also, 27 is my lucky number, and I made sure to have 27 chapters.

Thank you, Billie Joe Armstrong and Green Day, for showing me that being an "American Idiot", or in the "Minority," or the "Jesus of Suburbia," or feeling stuck in "The Static Age," is perfectly normal.

Thank you, Brandon Flowers and The Killers, for looking on the "Mr. Brightside," being "Human," getting me out of a "Rut" and "For Reasons Unknown…"

Thank you, Adam Levine and Maroon 5, for showing me the "Daylight" and picking me up in dark times through music, especially on "Sunday Morning."

Thank you, Ernie Johnson, for being the consummate human and professional, and one of the greatest humanitarians in the world. "Be a better human. How are you going to do it?" – EJ

Thank you, Chris Pratt, for redefining yourself at a time in your life when I was at a turning point in mine.

Thank you, Adam Sandler, for all the Hanukkah Songs, and a comedy about an Israeli soldier that is also somehow an extremely honest, optimistic view on the Israel-Palestine conflict.

Thank you, Seth MacFarlane, for holding nothing back in the service of entertainment and laughter. You are my *Family Guy* and my *American Dad*.

Thank you, Hunter Pence, for effortlessly mixing nerd culture with the sports world and being a great teammate.

Thank you, Gordon Hayward, for the wristband. I still wear it. "Eyes up, do the work."

Thank you, Conan O'Brien, for being more than a talk show host. The *Conan* show had heart, it had laughs, and it felt like a second family with Andy, Sona, Jimmy V and whatever various tasks and duties Jordan had.

Thank you, *That '70s Show*, for being relentlessly optimistic and innocent in a time when we are struggling with both.

Thank you, Charles Barkley, for perfectly mixing the art of sports and entertainment, with an emphasis on the latter.

Thank you, Mrs. King, Mr. Arend, Mr. Thomson, Mr. Thompson, Mrs. Ford, Mrs. Heck, Coach Walta, Coach Brown, Professor Bagley, Professor Loftis and many more for showing me the power of a good teacher and inspiring me to make the same impact.

Thank you to all those I met in treatment: fellow patients, counselors and doctors. Knowing I wasn't alone in my fight against OCD was the biggest step in my recovery process. This book is for a lot of people, but it is ultimately for anyone with OCD or affected by OCD.

POST-CREDITS: 2022 – THE OTHER SIDE

When Samuel L. Jackson showed up as Nick Fury at the end of *Iron Man*, the Marvel Cinematic Universe officially put their signature post-credits scenes into motion.

Sure, the MCU didn't invent the post-credits scene, but perhaps they perfected the art of building anticipation and hype for serial storytelling.

I guess I'll give it a try.

***

I started writing *I'm So OCD* in 2018 and finished it during an inspired ten-hour writing frenzy on a rare snowy Texas day in early 2022.

I intended to end the story with my college graduation, and originally, I had no post-credits scene. I sent an early copy of the book to four people: Dr. Robinson, Dr. Abel and my parents.

My dad said he liked it, *but* that I should (literally) bookend this thing with at least some of what I accomplished *after* 2020. I was hesitant, feeling I had told the parts of my life story I wanted to tell and had emotionally closed this book, both literally and figuratively.

He made a great point, saying I owed it to the readers to let them know that I had come out of all this a winner.

***

The date is April 16, 2022. It's Saturday, there's no school, and I'm half-watching a Dallas Mavericks-Utah Jazz playoff game in an

NBA I don't recognize, thinking about how, in years past, a Mavs home playoff game would mean I'd be there in person with my dad.

Times have changed.

I've also got an article open about how Warner Bros. movies are now under new ownership for what seems like the fifth time this century. Like always, I'm multitasking. A game is on, and the laptop is open. Even the phone is out.

I'm in my Frisco apartment, on the couch under a blanket, and for lunch I just had a roast beef sandwich with mustard that I threw together in a minute. I might have a drink soon.

I'm a little numb to it all, wishing I could enjoy any of these various lifestyle choices a little more.

Fun post-credits scene, right? It's like the Avengers eating shawarma after the Battle of New York. That was a last-minute inclusion, just like this.

I admit that I'm bored. But I'm used to this. I've spent most of my life, especially since mental illness and OCD became a part of it in 2006, alone. It's a weird sort of familiar that I've gotten too used to.

I promise there's a "but" coming. And here it is. Here's the good news:

I am healthy. I am independent. Most importantly, I am happy.

Sure, I'm bored, but I like my life, and that's something that seemed very impossible for the longest time and eluded me for more than a decade.

Yes, I am happy. I love my job. I love teaching. I really do. I'm happy to be independent and in charge of my own life. But the key ingredient of it all, at least to me, is that I love my job.

I love teaching. I love the kids. They give me a purpose and an energy every day that I don't know that I would have without them.

My anxiety is as improved as my OCD, but both still linger. I still battle severe depression, but I'm at my best when I'm at work and around the kids. The best therapy for me is to bury myself in my work, and thankfully, my work is to fulfill my purpose as an educator and leader of young people.

There are good days and bad days, but overall, I am happy. What more could you ask for?

Well, in a few months, I'm hitting the reset button.

***

I've lived at home my whole life. Almost literally.

I spent half of my college career commuting from home. I lived at home during the pandemic. Technically, I've lived in Houston for many nonconsecutive months, but I was with my parents or a parent all but one time.

I *was* on my own in Boston, but that wasn't the best of circumstances.

The past year, I lived in an apartment in Frisco, 15 minutes from my parents' home in Plano.

Outside of these exceptions, I've lived my whole life with my parents. It was for obvious medical reasons, but there's a part of me that has always wanted to get out.

And this summer, that's exactly what I'll be doing.

I'm happy with where my life is, but I still feel as if my life has never really been my own. I've relied on others since the day I was born, only very recently obtaining a semblance of true independence.

It feels good, but like Anakin Skywalker and his quest for ultimate power, I want more.

So, this summer, I'm picking up what little baggage I have – clothes, my PlayStation, and I guess some hats? – and moving to Arizona.

The exact location will be determined by the job I get, and I will still be teaching and coaching. On the job front, I've found my passion. But I want to explore a little more of the world, and soon, I'll be doing just that.

***

It's been a long, strange trip, as they say. It's been a lot of work. A lot of sweat and tears, but I've got one life and I'm going to live it how I want, even if I missed my teenage years and got a late start on this whole adulthood thing.

No matter where I go, my history follows. All the life lessons, all the wonderful people. All the memories, good and bad. It's all there.

If I leave you with anything, I suppose it should be this.

In your darkest moments, your lowest times, on your worst days, remember: *There is hope.*

Don't lose hope.

I'm so OCD, and here I am.

ABOUT THE AUTHOR

Asher was born in Dallas, Texas, and raised in Plano. From a young age, he wanted to be a professional athlete, movie star or singer in a band – you know, normal stuff.

Whatever far-fetched dreams he had were shattered when mental illness entered his life at age 12. As he slowly regained his health over a decade-plus of hard work and hospital stays, he focused on a career in sports journalism and broadcasting, most notably working for the Frisco RoughRiders, Texas Legends, Dallas Mavericks and Texas Rangers. He eventually changed course and now teaches middle school social studies and coaches youth baseball and basketball teams in Phoenix, Arizona.

When he's not busy working, he loves to watch movies, especially *Star Wars* (pre-*The Last Jedi*), Marvel (up until *Avengers: Endgame*) and the Christopher Nolan Batman trilogy.

Follow Asher on Instagram and Facebook @asherfeltman.

RESOURCES

It's okay to not be okay. Help is never far away.

The OCD Foundation:
https://iocdf.org/

988 Suicide & Crisis Lifeline:
https://988lifeline.org/
or dial 988

Mental health tips and support:
https://www.mentalhealth.gov/get-help/immediate-help

When I started writing this book, I had no idea that the Houston OCD Program had been bought by McLean, but my story connects in so many ways that this shouldn't surprise me. Here is their link:

https://www.mcleanhospital.org/treatment/ocd-houston

***

Thanks again, Mom and Dad. Again – in no particular order.

RESOURCES

ABOUT CHERISH EDITIONS

Cherish Editions is a bespoke self-publishing service for authors of mental health, well-being and inspirational books.

As a division of Trigger Publishing, the UK's leading independent mental health and well-being publisher, we are experienced in creating and selling positive, responsible, important and inspirational books, which work to de-stigmatize the issues around mental health and improve the mental health and well-being of those who read our titles.

Founded by Adam Shaw, a mental health advocate, author and philanthropist, and leading psychologist Lauren Callaghan, Cherish Editions aims to publish books that provide advice, support and inspiration. We nurture our authors so that their stories can unfurl on the page, helping them to share their uplifting and moving stories.

Cherish Editions is unique in that a percentage of the profits from the sale of our books goes directly to leading mental health charity Shawmind, to deliver its vision to provide support for those experiencing mental ill health.

Find out more about Cherish Editions by visiting cherisheditions.com or joining us on:
Twitter @cherisheditions
Facebook @cherisheditions
Instagram @cherisheditions

ABOUT SHAWMIND

A proportion of profits from the sale of all Trigger books go to their sister charity, Shawmind, also founded by Adam Shaw and Lauren Callaghan. The charity aims to ensure that everyone has access to mental health resources whenever they need them.

Find out more about the work Shawmind do by visiting shawmind.org or joining them on:
Twitter @Shawmind_
Facebook @ShawmindUK
Instagram @Shawmind_

CPSIA information can be obtained
at www.ICGtesting.com
Printed in the USA
BVHW031656230323
661023BV00013B/213